Unlocking Rental Wealth

Strategies for Successful Property Investment and Management

Taylor Reed

Table of Contents

INTRODUCTION

Investing in rental properties is a proven path to building long-term wealth. In "Unlocking Rental Wealth: Strategies for Successful Property Investment and Management," you will find comprehensive guidance tailored for novice and seasoned investors. This book provides a step-by-step roadmap to navigate the complexities of property investment, from understanding market dynamics to selecting suitable properties and securing financing.

Beginning with the fundamentals, you'll learn to conduct thorough market research, identify lucrative investment opportunities, and assess property values. The book then delves into the intricacies of financing, offering strategies to secure the best mortgage rates and explore creative funding options.

Once you've acquired a property, discover effective renovation techniques to enhance its value and master the art of marketing to attract quality tenants. Detailed chapters on tenant management and property maintenance ensure you can smoothly handle everything from lease agreements to emergency repairs.

Legal considerations are crucial in property management, and this guide covers essential landlord-tenant laws, helping you stay compliant and protect your investments. As you grow more confident, explore advanced strategies to maximize returns and expand your portfolio sustainably.

With practical advice, real-world examples, and actionable strategies, "Unlocking Rental Wealth" equips you with the knowledge and tools needed to succeed in the competitive rental property investment and management world.

CHAPTER I

Understanding the Basics of Rental Property Investment

What is rental property investment?

Investing in rental properties is the practice of buying homes to rent to rent them out to tenants to provide a reliable source of income. Long-term supporters of this investment approach include people looking to accumulate wealth and become financially independent. Purchasing residential or commercial properties, managing them well, and eventually benefiting from property appreciation and rental revenue are the fundamental components of investment in rental properties.

The ability to generate two streams of income is the main attraction of investing in rental properties. First, the money is received directly from renters who submit monthly rent payments. If the property is well-maintained and in a desired area, this revenue can be a dependable source of cash flow. The possibility of long-term capital appreciation is the second. An investor's equity in a property increases as its value rises over time, increasing their net worth overall.

The relative stability of rental property investments, as opposed to other investment types like stocks or cryptocurrencies, is one of their main benefits. Because real estate markets are typically less erratic, investing in them is more predictable and safer. Because of their consistency, rental properties are desirable for cautious investors who want to achieve modest growth while preserving cash.

It's essential to comprehend the many kinds of rental properties that are out there before investing in rental houses. Investors frequently select residential properties, such as apartment buildings, single-family homes, and multi-family units. Every kind has particular advantages and difficulties. For example, single-family homes usually draw long-term tenants and don't require as much management. In contrast, multi-family properties might rent for more money but can need more management involvement. Another option for investing is in commercial real estate, which includes office buildings, retail establishments, and industrial properties. These assets frequently give better returns but need more significant initial investment and in-depth commercial real estate market knowledge.

Undertaking extensive market research is the first step to becoming a profitable rental property investor. It might be beneficial to recognize profitable investment opportunities to understand local real estate trends, economic indicators, and demographic movements. This entails examining job growth, population rates, and neighborhood features that draw in tenants. A thorough market analysis can identify new communities with significant development potential, enabling investors to place their money in places with considerable rental demand and an increase in property value.

Choosing the ideal property is the next stage when a potential market has been found. This entails assessing possible properties according to attributes, including location, state, and rental potential. Location is crucial since homes in sought-after areas with top-notch schools, convenient access to the city, and other amenities typically draw in premium renters and fetch higher rentals. Another critical factor is the state of the property; well-maintained homes attract more potential tenants and require less immediate renovation expenditure.

Obtaining funding is yet another essential component of investing in rental properties. A variety of funding solutions, including conventional mortgages, private loans, and partnerships, must be negotiated by investors. It is crucial to comprehend credit ratings and how they affect loan terms to obtain advantageous financing. Furthermore, innovative financing techniques like seller financing or using equity in already-owned properties can offer different ways to buy rental properties.

The buying process entails several processes, such as haggling with sellers, doing due diligence by evaluating and inspecting the property and finalizing the agreement. To ensure that the investment is sound and that there are no unforeseen problems that could affect profitability, each process demands close attention to detail.

Effective property management becomes essential after a property is purchased. This covers everything, from managing tenant relations and upkeep to advertising the property to draw in renters. Effective property management ensures that the rental income is maximized, the property is kept in good condition, and the renters are happy. Attracting excellent tenants primarily depends on marketing methods, including making attractive rental listings, using online platforms, and charging competitive rental costs.

Maximizing returns is the ultimate objective of investing in rental properties. This entails using property appreciation and steady rental revenue generation to create long-term wealth. An investor's portfolio expansion becomes a realistic approach as they acquire experience and confidence. Investing in diverse properties and locations reduces risk and increases total profits. Furthermore, more sophisticated tactics like tax preparation, rent optimization, and property upgrades can increase revenue even more.

A thorough manual for navigating the complicated world of rental properties, Understanding the Fundamentals of Rental Property Investment gives insightful advice and doable tactics for success. This book gives you the information and resources to realize the full potential of investing in rental properties, regardless of your experience level.

Benefits of investing in rental properties

Several advantages make investing in rental homes desirable for anyone looking to accumulate wealth and ensure financial stability. The possibility of a consistent passive income stream is among the most alluring benefits. As tenants pay rent, rental properties can produce a consistent income flow each month, unlike other investment vehicles that could need ongoing care and supervision. This revenue often leaves a surplus that can be reinvested or utilized to augment the investor's other sources of income. It can also pay the mortgage, taxes, and maintenance fees associated with the property. The foundation of a well-balanced investment strategy is rental income due to its stability and dependability.

The possibility of long-term appreciation is a significant advantage of investing in rental homes. Property values usually rise with market demand and inflation in real estate markets, which tend to expand over time. This appreciation may result in significant gains when the property is finally sold. Well-selected rental properties in prime locations tend to hold their value better than other asset classes, even during market turbulence. Additionally, by taking out loans against their equity, investors can leverage their properties and grow their portfolios and returns without liquidating their holdings.

Tax advantages mainly influence the appeal of investing in rental properties. Several tax deductions are offered to real estate investors that are unavailable to other investors. Some of these deductions include interest on mortgages, property taxes, operating costs, depreciation, and repair charges. Especially when it comes to depreciation, investors can lower their taxable income by considering the property's deterioration over time—even when its actual value may increase. These tax advantages can significantly improve the net return on rental property investment.

Leverage is another benefit of rental properties; it enables investors to buy homes with a low down payment and finance the remaining amount with a mortgage. Because rental income and appreciation depend on the entire property's worth rather than the investor's initial equity, this leverage increases the returns on investment. Rental properties are an effective means of accumulating wealth because, for example, an investor can hold a sizable asset and reap the benefits of its full appreciation potential if they put down 20% of the property's value and finance the remaining 80%.

Another essential advantage of investing in rental properties is diversification. Real estate is an asset class that frequently behaves differently from stocks and bonds, which helps distribute risk over a more extensive range of investments. Because real estate markets may continue to grow or even stabilize when other markets do not, this diversification can shield investors from market downturns. Furthermore, rental properties might bring in money during recessions, protecting the portfolio from losses in other sectors.

More control is another benefit of investing in rental properties over other kinds of investments. Real estate investors have direct control over their assets, whereas stock market investors are at the mercy of the market and the choices made by corporate executives. They can make calculated choices about rental pricing, tenant selection, improvements, and property management. With this power, investors may react proactively to shifting market conditions and directly affect how well their investment performs.

Lastly, purchasing rental property has the potential to have a positive social and community influence. Investors can enhance renters' living conditions and support community redevelopment by building high-quality homes. This may result from positive social effects, including higher property values, lower crime rates, and improved communal well-being. In addition to the financial rewards, moral landlords who take good care of their properties and treat their tenants properly can significantly impact their communities.

To sum up, there are a lot of different advantages to investing in rental homes. They provide substantial tax benefits, the potential for long-term appreciation, and a dependable passive income stream. Their attractiveness is further increased by their capacity to leverage investments, attain portfolio diversification, and maintain asset control. In addition, rental properties offer the chance for beneficial social effect, the tangible asset of a physical asset, and a hedge against inflation. Investing in rental properties is an appealing option for individuals wishing to accumulate and maintain wealth over time because of these benefits. Whether you're a first-time investor or a seasoned real estate tycoon, strategically acquiring and managing rental properties can be essential to reaching your financial objectives and building a prosperous future.

Types of rental properties (single-family, multi-family, commercial, etc.)

Before investing, it's essential to comprehend the several kinds of rental properties, each with its benefits and drawbacks. Single-family homes, multi-family apartments, and commercial properties are the most popular categories of rental properties. Investors must match their property selections with their financial objectives and management skills because each category presents unique opportunities and calls for various management strategies.

Single-family homes may be the most common kind of rental property. Like families looking for stability and solitude, long-term renters are often drawn to these stand-alone residential homes. Compared to more extensive multi-family or commercial properties, single-family homes usually have lower initial expenses, making them more affordable for novice investors. Furthermore, single-family houses typically require less intense maintenance and tend to draw in better-maintained tenants because there is only one tenant or family to handle. A single-family rental's revenue is confined to a single source; therefore, vacancies can significantly affect cash flow.

Conversely, duplexes, triplexes, quadplexes, and more significant apartment buildings are multi-family properties. These properties benefit from several tenants living under one roof, providing a variety of revenue streams. Rent from other units can keep a continuous revenue flow even if one property is unoccupied. Multi-family properties can be more affordable because maintenance and repairs may be divided more effectively among numerous units. For instance, a single HVAC system or roof replacement can serve several occupants. Nonetheless, multi-family property management can be more difficult and complex, needing excellent people and organizational abilities to manage the demands and concerns of several tenants at once.

Commercial rental properties include office buildings, retail establishments, industrial assets, and mixed-use developments. Because of their commercial character and larger scale of operations, these properties usually yield better rental income when compared to residential properties. Businesses frequently use commercial spaces as tenants, which may result in longer lease terms and more consistent revenue. Furthermore, to lessen the financial strain on the landlord, commercial leases frequently contain provisions requiring renters to pay for all or part of the upkeep, insurance, and property taxes associated with the property. Commercial real estate, however, entails more significant risks and necessitates a better comprehension of the industry. They may have lengthier vacancies between renters and usually require a more substantial initial investment.

Vacation rentals are just another subset of rental properties. These homes are usually found in well-known tourist locations and are leased out to travelers for a brief period. Vacation rentals can produce high rental income, especially during the busiest travel seasons. Vacation rental management and reaching a worldwide audience have become more accessible for investors thanks to platforms like VRBO and Airbnb. Vacation rentals necessitate rigorous management, regular cleaning, and marketing initiatives to sustain high occupancy rates.

Additionally, they are vulnerable to seasonal variations, which may produce erratic revenue sources.

Another niche rental sector is student housing, which consists of homes designed for college students. These homes are usually found close to colleges and institutions, giving students easy access to housing options. Due to the high demand in college cities and the option to charge rent by the room rather than the unit, investing in student housing is profitable. However, because students typically rent for the academic year, student housing frequently has more excellent turnover rates. It can require more upkeep and administration due to the lifestyle and behavior of the renter demographic.

Apart from the aforementioned basic types, specialty rental properties include co-living spaces and mobile home parks. In addition to offering reasonably priced housing options, mobile home parks can produce steady income with little upkeep. In metropolitan regions, co-living spaces have become more and more popular. They serve young professionals and students looking for flexible and economical living options. These real estate assets provide communal living areas with separate rental agreements for bedrooms, fostering a feeling of the neighborhood while optimizing rental yield.

Investors who want to diversify their holdings and optimize profits must understand the many kinds of rental properties. Every property has its advantages and difficulties, necessitating varying degrees of administration, investment, and market expertise. Investors can utilize the qualities of each property type to create a solid and lucrative rental property portfolio by matching their property selections with their investment strategy and risk tolerance. Careful investment in rental properties can pave the path to long-term financial success, whether one chooses the familiarity of single-family houses, the income diversity of multi-family units, the high returns of commercial properties, or the specialty vacation and student housing opportunities.

Key terms and concepts in real estate

Anyone attempting to navigate the complicated world of real estate investment must have a solid understanding of the fundamental phrases and concepts in the field. These fundamentals give the industry its language and the structure required to make well-informed judgments. Property itself, broadly divided into residential, commercial, industrial, and land categories, is the fundamental idea behind real estate. Commercial properties include office buildings, retail stores, and hotels; residential properties include single-family homes, apartments, and condos. Land can be developed for commercial, residential, or agricultural purposes or left undeveloped as industrial assets for manufacturing and storage.

A key idea in real estate is location, sometimes summed up with the expression "location, location, location." The value and desirability of a property are greatly influenced by its location. The quality of the nearby schools, the accessibility of public transit, the neighborhood's safety, and the proximity to facilities all affect the location. The price at which a property would sell under typical circumstances, with neither the buyer nor the seller acting under undue pressure, is known as market or fair market value. This is not the same as appraised value, which is established by a qualified appraiser who evaluates the property's value based on several criteria, such as similar transactions and the state of the property.

Another crucial concept is equity, which is the difference between the current market value of the property and the mortgage balance. Gaining equity over time can improve an investor's capacity to borrow money and maintain stability. The idea of leverage, which entails leveraging borrowed money—like a mortgage—to boost the possible return on investment, is closely connected. With very little personal wealth, leverage enables investors to control more significant assets, increasing potential benefits and hazards.

The net amount of money coming into and going out of a rental property is known as cash flow. There is positive cash flow when rental income surpasses outlays for things like maintenance, insurance, taxes, and mortgage payments. Conversely, negative cash flow occurs when expenses exceed rental income, which may indicate a risk to investors. The capitalization rate, often the cap rate, is another crucial financial indicator. It calculates the rate of return on an investment in real estate by considering the anticipated revenue the property will produce. Net operating income (NOI) is divided by the property's purchase price or current market value to determine the cap rate.

A critical measure of a property's profitability is its net operating income (NOI), which is the revenue produced by the asset after operating expenditures are subtracted but before taxes and financing charges are subtracted. Operating expenses include maintenance, utilities, insurance, and property management fees. Conversely, gross rental revenue is the whole amount received from rent before any costs are subtracted. Investors can assess the financial stability of their investments by being aware of these words.

Local restrictions, known as zoning laws, specify the permitted uses for properties within particular geographic zones. It is imperative for investors, particularly those contemplating construction or modifications to property usage, to comprehend these rules since they can impact property value and potential uses. For example, zoned land can only be used commercially with the local government's approval.

In an escrow agreement, the money needed for a transaction between two parties is held by a third party who also controls the payment of that money. Holding the money in a secure escrow account that is only released until all contract conditions are fulfilled helps to ensure a safe transaction.

When a borrower defaults on a loan, the lender may foreclose** and take possession of the property to recoup the unpaid balance. Investors who may explore buying foreclosed properties, which can occasionally be obtained at a bargain but may come with added dangers and problems, must thoroughly understand foreclosure laws and processes.

Real estate agents and brokers are professionals who help with property purchases, sales, and rentals. Agents help clients navigate the real estate market and usually report to brokers. Since they have received additional training and certification, brokers can work independently and oversee other agents.

Real estate agents trade listings and obtain information about properties for sale through a database called the Multiple Listing Service (MLS). It gives real estate brokers and agents a consolidated platform to search for properties and market listings, with significant benefits regarding exposure and accurate information.

Anyone hoping to succeed in the real estate industry must comprehend these fundamental terminology and ideas. They offer the basic information needed to assess prospects, make wise decisions, and handle the intricacies of real estate investing. Gaining success and optimizing the potential of your assets requires that you understand this jargon, regardless of your level of experience or interest in real estate.

CHAPTER II

Market Research and Property Selection

Importance of market research

A vital component of a profitable real estate investment strategy is market research. Its significance is immeasurable since it gives investors essential information about the workings of the real estate market, enabling them to make well-informed decisions and reduce risks. Fundamentally, market research entails systematically gathering and examining information about several facets of the real estate industry, such as economic markers, demographic patterns, and characteristics unique to individual properties. Investors can spot profitable possibilities, steer clear of potential hazards, and eventually reach their financial objectives by comprehending these components.

The capacity to make well-informed selections is the main advantage of market research for real estate investors. Investors who need a thorough understanding of the market are effectively operating unthinkingly, making decisions based only on their intuition or on insufficient information. With the help of market research, investors may get a clear picture of the situation and predict future trends and movements. Analyzing variables important in determining property valuations and prospective rental revenue include local economic conditions, employment rates, population growth, and housing demand.

AA's crucial component of market research is a grasp of the economic variables that impact real estate markets. These include inflation, interest rates, and the state of the economy. Low interest rates, for example, usually make borrowing more affordable, encouraging the acquisition of real estate and raising prices. On the other hand, high interest rates may reduce demand and cause price drops. Similar to how purchasing power and property values are impacted by inflation, a healthy housing market is frequently associated with a strong economy and high employment rates. Investors can time purchases and sales to optimize returns by monitoring these indications.

Trends in demographics are yet another essential aspect of market research. Gaining knowledge about a region's population dynamics, including age distribution, income distribution, and migration trends, can be extremely helpful in determining the need for housing. For instance, there is frequently a greater demand for rental houses in places with a noticeable increase in the population, especially among younger people of working age. However, there can be a greater need for senior housing choices or downsizing in areas with an aging population. Investors can efficiently meet market demand by positioning themselves in line with demographic trends.

Real estate investing is always influenced by location, and market research can assist in identifying the most incredible places to put money down. Only some cities or areas are equal, and location can significantly impact property values. Analyzing variables, including accessibility to facilities (schools, parks, and shopping malls), transit connections, crime rates, and future development plans, are all part of market research. Higher-quality renters and higher-paying rentals are typically drawn to properties in desirable areas with top-notch schools and low crime rates. Furthermore, places with planned economic or infrastructure developments may have a high potential for appreciation.

A grasp of the competitors is another essential component of market research. Analyzing the dynamics of supply and demand in the local market is required. Investors can determine opportunities and hazards by evaluating market saturation by analyzing the quantity of available properties and the rate at which they are rented or sold. For example, an oversupplied market with many rental units and low occupancy rates may indicate better moments to invest in that location. On the other hand, a market with strong demand and little supply may present fantastic chances for capital gains from rentals and real estate.

A crucial component of market research is carrying out a comparative market analysis (CMA). To calculate a CMA, comparable homes in the same neighborhood that have either recently sold or are presently for sale are compared to the property of interest. By determining a property's fair market worth, this comparison helps investors avoid overpaying and ensures they can anticipate competitive rental rates. It also aids in locating homes that are inexpensive or have the potential to yield more significant profits because of unique attributes or upgrades.

Features unique to a given property must also be considered during market research. These include the property's state, dimensions, design, and unique qualities that might draw purchasers or tenants. Investors should also evaluate the cost of essential upgrades or repairs, as they can affect the investment's overall profitability. An extensive examination of the property and an analysis of maintenance records can reveal possible problems and long-term expenses.

Comprehending the legal and regulatory landscape is an additional vital component of market research. The laws and rules that control the real estate industry include construction codes, zoning legislation, and rental policies. These have the potential to affect an investment's viability and profitability significantly. Strict rent control laws, for example, may restrict the amount charged for rentals, and zoning regulations may limit the kinds of renovations that can be done to a property. Investors can avoid legal hazards and make compliant, profitable judgments by keeping current on these requirements.

In addition to these variables, future market trends and developments should also be considered in market research. This entails staying current on local and national real estate news, economic projections, and new technology that may affect the market. For instance, the increase in remote employment has changed the market for housing, with more people looking for homes in rural or suburban locations. By keeping up with these trends, investors may adjust their tactics and take advantage of new possibilities as they present themselves.

Evaluating an investment's financial viability is another benefit of market research. Investors can compute possible returns and ascertain whether a property fits their investment criteria by examining data such as rental yields, property appreciation rates, and expense ratios. Projecting cash flows, figuring out ROI, and comprehending the tax ramifications of property ownership are all part of this financial research. A comprehensive economic analysis guarantees that investors may attain their targeted profit margins and are not surprised by unforeseen expenses.

To sum up, market research is essential to a profitable real estate investment. It offers the knowledge required to manage the complexity of the real estate industry, match investments with market demand, and make well-informed judgments. Investors can reduce risks and optimize returns by being fully aware of economic statistics, demographic trends, location variables, competition, property characteristics, legal requirements, and upcoming developments. Thorough market research is essential to realizing the maximum return on your real estate investments, regardless of your experience level.

How to analyze local real estate markets

Analyzing local real estate markets is critical for anyone looking to invest in property, whether you are a seasoned investor or a first-time buyer. A comprehensive market analysis provides insights into the dynamics of the area, helping investors make informed decisions and minimize risks. This process involves evaluating various factors, including economic indicators, demographic trends, housing supply and demand, property values, rental rates, and local regulations.

The first step in analyzing a local real estate market is to assess the broader economic conditions. Local economies can vary significantly from one area to another, and understanding these differences is crucial. Economic indicators include employment rates, income levels, and economic growth. A thriving local economy with low unemployment and rising incomes typically correlates with a robust real estate market, as more people can afford to buy or rent properties. Conversely, areas with high unemployment and stagnant wages may indicate weaker housing demand.

Demographic trends are another vital component of market analysis. Population growth, age distribution, and household formation rates can significantly impact real estate markets. Areas experiencing population growth often see increased demand for housing, driving up property values and rental rates.

Analyzing the age distribution helps identify target demographics; for example, a growing number of young professionals may increase demand for rental apartments, while an aging population might drive the need for senior housing.

Understanding household formation rates, such as the number of new households created, provides insights into future housing demand. Location is a perennial factor in real estate, and analyzing local market conditions involves a detailed examination of neighborhood characteristics.

Proximity to amenities such as schools, parks, shopping centers, and public transportation can significantly influence property values. Safe neighborhoods with good schools are typically more desirable, attracting families willing to pay a premium for these benefits. Additionally, areas undergoing revitalization or development, such as constructing new infrastructure or commercial projects, can offer significant appreciation potential.

Investors should consider both current amenities and planned future developments when evaluating locations. Supply and demand dynamics are central to understanding local real estate markets. Analyzing the current inventory of available properties and the rate at which they are being sold or rented helps gauge market saturation.

A market with a high supply of properties and low demand might indicate an oversupply, leading to downward pressure on prices and rental rates. Conversely, a market with limited supply and high demand can drive up prices and rents, offering the potential for higher returns.

Understanding the absorption rate, which measures how quickly properties are sold or rented, provides insights into the market's health and the balance between supply and demand.

Property values and price trends are essential aspects of market analysis. Historical data on property values helps identify trends and predict future movements. Analyzing median home prices, price per square foot, and year-over-year appreciation rates provides a clear picture of the market's trajectory.

Rising property values indicate a strong market, while declining values may signal potential problems. It's also essential to compare property values across neighborhoods within the same market to identify areas with better investment potential. Rental rates and rental yield are critical for investors interested in rental properties.

Analyzing current rental rates and comparing them to property values helps determine the rental yield, the annual rental income expressed as a percentage of the property's purchase price. A high rental yield indicates a potentially profitable investment, while a low yield might suggest that the property is overpriced relative to the rental income it can generate. Understanding vacancy rates is also crucial; high ones can signal an oversaturated rental market, while low rates indicate strong demand. Local regulations and zoning laws can significantly impact real estate investments. Each municipality has its own set of rules governing land use, property development, and rental regulations. Understanding these regulations is essential to avoid legal pitfalls and ensure compliance. Zoning laws determine what types of properties can be built in specific areas, which can affect a property's potential uses and value. For instance, an investor looking to develop multi-family housing must ensure the property is zoned for such use.

Additionally, rental regulations, such as rent control laws, can impact rental income and profitability. Tax implications are another essential consideration when analyzing local real estate markets. Property taxes vary widely from jurisdiction to jurisdiction and can significantly affect the property's cost. High property taxes can erode rental income and overall profitability, while areas with lower taxes may offer better investment returns. Investors should also consider any available tax incentives or deductions, such as those for historic properties, energy-efficient upgrades, or investment in designated opportunity zones. Engaging with local real estate professionals can provide valuable insights into the market. Real estate agents, brokers, property managers, and appraisers have firsthand knowledge of local market conditions and can offer guidance based on their experience. Networking with these professionals can help investors better understand market trends, property values, and investment opportunities.

Additionally, local government offices and real estate associations often publish market reports and data that can be useful for analysis. Technology and online resources have made market analysis more accessible than ever. Real estate websites and platforms provide a wealth of data, including property listings, sales history, rental rates, and neighborhood statistics. Tools such as heat maps, visually representing data like crime rates or school quality, can help investors quickly assess different areas. These resources allow investors to conduct thorough market research from anywhere, complementing on-the-ground observations and professional advice.

In conclusion, analyzing local real estate markets involves comprehensively evaluating economic conditions, demographic trends, neighborhood characteristics, supply and demand dynamics, property values, rental rates, and local regulations. This multifaceted approach provides the insights to make informed investment decisions and maximize returns. Whether investing in residential, commercial, or rental properties, understanding the local market is critical to identifying opportunities, mitigating risks, and achieving long-term success in real estate investment. By leveraging traditional methods and modern technology, investors can gain a detailed and nuanced understanding of the markets they are interested in, positioning themselves for successful investments.

Identifying promising locations for investment
Finding good places to invest in real estate is essential to success in the real estate industry. A property's valuation, prospective rental income, and chances for appreciation are greatly influenced by its location. A favorable mix of characteristics, including infrastructure development, population trends, economic conditions, and quality of life, make an area for investments highly promising. By comprehending and evaluating these components, Investors can identify regions with the most excellent chances for lucrative investments.

One of the primary markers of a region's potential as a desirable place to invest is its economic health. High real estate markets are usually found in areas with high economic growth, low unemployment rates, and growing income levels. Given the current state of the economy, more individuals can afford to buy or rent real estate, which will increase demand and raise property values. Investors should seek out areas with various expanding businesses, as they offer stability and opportunities for long-term growth. For example, cities with booming healthcare, education, or technology industries frequently draw a continual stream of professionals, increasing housing demand.

Promising investment sites are identified in large part by considering demographic patterns. One crucial aspect is population growth; areas that see a surge in newcomers frequently have higher housing demand, which drives up property values and rental rates. Investors need to consider the age distribution as well. While older populations may offer prospects for elder housing or assisted living facilities, areas with a high concentration of young professionals may see a greater demand for rental units. Furthermore, knowing household formation rates—the number of new households—can help predict future housing requirements.

Finding attractive places to invest is also influenced by the state of the infrastructure. This can significantly increase an area's attraction and investment in infrastructure, such as roads, airports, public transportation, and utilities. Property values typically grow in areas with ongoing or planned infrastructure developments as convenience and accessibility increase. For example, the building of a new highway or subway line can bring more businesses and residents to neighborhoods that were previously less accessible. Investors wishing to find locations primed for infrastructure enhancements can look into the plans and initiatives of local governments.

Quality of life is a broad but crucial factor to consider while assessing potential investment sites. Area desirability is influenced by several factors, including general safety, recreational opportunities, healthcare accessibility, and the caliber of the neighborhood's schools. Good schools and safe neighborhoods are frequently top priorities for families, which increases demand in these locations. Similarly, an area's appeal can be improved by having access to parks, cultural institutions, and entertainment venues. To guarantee consistent demand for real estate, investors ought to seek areas that provide a good standard of living.

Finding viable locations requires understanding the real estate industry's dynamics of supply and demand. Higher rental income and faster appreciation are expected in areas with a shortage of available homes due to high demand. Investors ought to examine the available property inventory, the amount of building going on, and the vacancy rates. Strong demand is indicated by a low vacancy rate, which implies that homes will probably be rented out promptly and reliably. On the other hand, high vacancy rates indicate an oversaturated market. Investors can discover markets with favorable conditions and assess the balance between supply and demand by thoroughly understanding these dynamics.

Knowing local real estate values and pricing trends is essential for locating potentially successful sites. Investors can identify patterns and predict future moves by examining past data on property values and current sales. Investment opportunities are typically best found in areas where property values have consistently increased. But it's also critical to recognize communities that could be underappreciated but have room to grow, frequently due to impending developments or bettering community circumstances. As they grow and mature, these emerging markets have the potential to yield substantial returns.

The possibility of rental revenue is crucial for investors concentrating on rental properties. The profitability of an investment can be ascertained by examining the rental yield and current rental rates. Stable and appealing revenue streams can be found in areas with strong demand and competitive rental rates. The area's affordability should be taken into account by investors as well. Higher rental yields are more likely to occur in areas where property values are comparatively low in rental revenue.

Zoning and local rules may affect how profitable and feasible real estate ventures are. Land use, development, and rental property regulations are specific to each jurisdiction. Investors need to be aware of these rules to stay out of trouble with the law and ensure their investment plans comply with local legislation. For example, zones that are conducive to multifamily housing or commercial constructions may present more options for a broader range of investment kinds. Additionally, estimating rental income and long-term viability requires an awareness of local rental laws and regulations, such as rent control.

Finding potential investment locations also involves taking tax issues into account. Regional variations in property taxes, income taxes, and other tax benefits can significantly impact investment results. Excessive property taxes can lower total profitability, while places that provide tax breaks for investments in specific zones or property upgrades can increase profits. Investors should assess a prospective investment location's tax climate to determine how it will affect their financial objectives.

When determining potential locations, market research and expert guidance are crucial. Speaking with nearby brokers, property managers, real estate agents, and other experts can provide information on the market's state, new trends, and undiscovered possibilities. These experts can give advice based on their expertise and knowledge since they are thoroughly aware of the regional market. Additionally, investors can undertake in-depth research and make data-driven judgments using online tools and resources, including real estate websites, market reports, and data analytics platforms.

To sum up, finding attractive places to invest in real estate requires a thorough examination of a variety of factors, including the state of the economy, demographic trends, infrastructure development, aspects of quality of life, market dynamics, property values, potential for rental income, local laws, and tax implications. Through combining these factors, expert analysis, and technology resources, investors can identify sectors with the most significant potential for long-term growth and financial gain. Choosing the ideal location is essential for optimizing profits and succeeding in the real estate market, regardless of whether one is investing in residential, commercial, or rental properties.

Assessing property value and potential for appreciation

To maximize profits and make well-informed decisions, real estate investors must evaluate their properties' worth and prospective appreciation. The term "property value" describes a property's monetary value at a specific moment, determined by several variables such as the property's location, amenities, size, condition, and market conditions. When assessing investment prospects and formulating successful strategies, it is essential to comprehend how these aspects influence value and project future appreciation potential.

A property's location is frequently mentioned as the most critical aspect influencing its value. Higher prices are usually associated with properties in well-liked communities with excellent schools, low crime rates, and easy access to amenities like parks, shopping centers, and public transit. Not only does being close to crucial job areas and transportation hubs improve accessibility and convenience for inhabitants, but it also adds value. A location's existing appeal, as well as possible future developments or infrastructure projects that could raise property values even further, should be taken into account by investors.

A key component of value assessment is property quality and condition. Properly maintained residences that have been upgraded with contemporary amenities and features tend to command higher prices and can support higher rental rates. On the other hand, homes in bad shape or needing significant renovations might fetch a lower price and need more funding to reach their full potential. Investors should perform comprehensive inspections and evaluations to effectively determine a property's condition and project the cost of any necessary modifications.

A property's size and layout can also affect its value. Though the value per square foot can vary significantly based on the market and region, larger homes usually fetch more incredible prices. Value is also influenced by how the property is laid up, how many bedrooms and baths it has, and how well-functioning its living areas are. Homes with adaptable floor plans that appeal to a broad spectrum of prospective tenants or buyers typically retain higher rental demand and resale values.

Features and amenities that improve inhabitants' quality of life can raise the value of a home. Modern kitchen and bathroom fixtures, energy-efficient windows, hardwood floors, and stainless steel appliances are some of these renovations. Extra features like community areas, fitness facilities, and swimming pools might draw in purchasers prepared to pay a premium in condominiums or planned developments. To optimize property value and appeal, investors should assess the cost and return on investment of adding or updating facilities.

Market conditions and trends heavily influence property value and potential appreciation. Markets for real estate can be cyclical, going through phases of sharp increases, stabilization, or even decreases. Investors can better grasp the state of the market and predict future changes by analyzing market patterns, including price and sales data from the past. Several factors, including an imbalance in supply and demand, interest rates, economic growth, and demographic changes, influence market circumstances that affect property values.

For investors looking to purchase properties with the potential to generate income, rental income potential is a crucial factor. Determining the property's financial sustainability and return on investment involves evaluating the prospective rental revenue of the purchase price. A sure indicator of profitability is rental yield, which is the annual rental revenue expressed as a percentage of the property's purchase price. While properties with lower yields could depend more on future appreciation for profitability, those with greater yields in comparison to market norms frequently offer superior income possibilities.

A property's potential for appreciation is determined by assessing the variables that can raise its value over time. These could include zoning modifications that permit increased density or commercial development, local infrastructural upgrades, and regional economic expansion. As demand rises and services get better, emerging neighborhoods and revitalized places can offer prospects for significant gain. Investors looking to find regions with potential for future gain can study economic indicators and municipal development plans.

Comparative market analysis (CMA) evaluation of nearby comparable properties is another step in determining a property's value. The fair market value of a property can be ascertained, and pricing patterns can be identified by comparing recent sales prices with the property's attributes. To determine competitive pricing and the desirability of a potential investment, investors should consider comparable properties that have recently sold and those that are presently for sale. Making data-driven decisions is aided by a comprehensive CMA, which offers insightful information about market conditions.

Legal and regulatory issues can impact property value and investment potential. Navigating possible limits or opportunities requires understanding local rules, building codes, and zoning laws governing property use and development. Tax ramifications, such as property taxes and any tax breaks for investments or renovation projects, should also be considered by investors. Evaluations for possible liabilities and compliance with environmental standards can also impact overall investment risk and property value.

In summary, determining a property's value and potential for appreciation necessitates a thorough assessment of its location, state, size, amenities, market conditions, potential for rental income, and regulatory factors. Real estate investors can make well-informed choices that optimize profits and minimize hazards through a methodical examination of these variables and the utilization of industry information and expert analysis. Achieving long-term success in the real estate market requires an awareness of the elements that determine property value and appreciation potential, regardless of whether one is investing in residential, commercial, or income-producing properties.

CHAPTER III

Financing Your Rental Property Investment

Overview of financing options (loans, mortgages, partnerships)

For real estate investors looking to maximize their investing strategies and purchase properties, having a solid understanding of financing choices is imperative. Availability and suitability of financing solutions might change depending on several variables, including market conditions, property type, and investor profile. This overview examines key financing options such as partnerships, mortgages, and conventional loans and their advantages, drawbacks, and possible effects on real estate investing.

A traditional bank loan is one of the most popular financing methods for real estate investing. These loans usually entail taking out a fixed amount from a bank or other financial organization, with conditions and interest rates determined by income, credit history, and property value. Bank loans come in fixed-rate or adjustable-rate mortgage structures and provide flexibility in repayment plans. While adjustable-rate mortgages (ARMs) offer lower introductory rates that change frequently based on market conditions, fixed-rate mortgages provide stability throughout the loan term with consistent monthly payments. Investors should thoroughly evaluate their financial standing and loan repayment capacity, considering possible variations in interest rates and rental income.

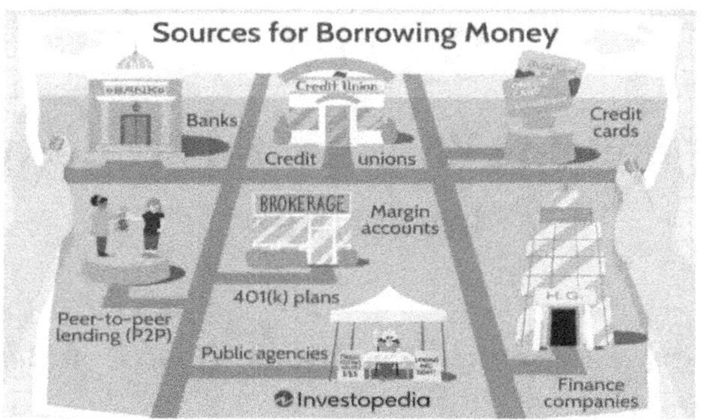

Another essential source of funding for real estate ventures is mortgages, especially for residential buildings. A mortgage is a loan that the real estate itself backs, and the lender retains a lien on the asset until the debt is paid back in full. Usually, a mortgage has terms between 15 and 30 years, and the collateral for the loan is the property. Although they can vary, down payments are frequently necessary to get good conditions and keep private mortgage insurance (PMI) expenses low. Investors can access various mortgage options, including government-backed mortgages like VA (Veterans Affairs) and FHA (Federal Housing Administration) loans, which may have less stringent credit requirements and lower down payment requirements. When evaluating mortgage options, one must compare fees, interest rates, and payback terms to identify the most economical option that meets investment objectives.

Several parties can pool resources and skills to finance real estate developments cooperatively through partnerships. There are many different types of partnerships. For example, limited partnerships are arrangements where investors supply funds without actively managing the property or joint ventures where participants share ownership and obligations. Through partnerships, one can share risk across several stakeholders, access more significant investment opportunities, and take advantage of various networks and skill sets. Successful partnerships necessitate precise agreements defining roles, duties, profit-sharing plans, and exit options to avoid conflicts and guarantee that interests are aligned. To protect their money, investors should thoroughly investigate possible partners and consult with legal counsel before drafting partnership agreements.

With loans coming from private lenders or individuals rather than financial institutions, private financing provides an alternative to conventional bank loans and mortgages. Investors with a credit history, a particular type of property, or other reasons that make traditional finance unattainable may find private financing appealing. Private lenders give greater flexibility in terms of loan terms, interest rates, and repayment schedules because they typically evaluate loan applications based on the potential and value of the property rather than strict credit requirements. However, because private funding carries more risk for lenders than standard loans, it could come with more outstanding fees and interest rates. Before moving further, investors should carefully review the terms and circumstances of private financing choices and consider the influence on overall investment returns.

Another popular type of private finance for real estate investment is hard money lending, especially for properties that need quick cash or short-term projects. Hard money lenders allow investors with little credit history or non-traditional sources of income to acquire loans based on the property's value rather than the borrower's creditworthiness. Compared to standard loans, hard money loans usually have lower loan-to-value ratios, higher interest rates, and shorter loan durations (usually 6 to 12 months). These loans are frequently utilized for purchases that must be made quickly to take advantage of investment possibilities, renovations, and fix-and-flip projects. Because hard money loans have more outstanding fees and shorter repayment terms, investors should carefully consider if their projects are profitable and feasible before using them.

In the real estate sector, peer-to-peer lending platforms and crowdfunding have become cutting-edge financing methods that use technology to link capital providers and investors. Through online platforms, crowdfunding enables various investors to pool their funds to support real estate projects, providing chances to invest in multiple properties at different investment sizes. Investors have two options: debt crowdfunding, in which investors offer loans secured by real estate, or equity crowdfunding, in which investors have ownership holdings in the property and may make profits. Peer-to-peer lending platforms offer flexible terms and affordable interest rates by facilitating direct loans between individual investors and borrowers, circumventing traditional financial institutions. These platforms make real estate investing and diversification opportunities accessible but require rigorous due diligence about platform laws, property evaluations, and project sponsors.

To sum up, real estate investors must carefully consider their financing options to successfully manage financial risks, maximize investment opportunities, and secure cash. Every form of funding—traditional loans, mortgages, partnerships, private equity, hard money loans, crowdsourcing, and peer-to-peer lending—has advantages, drawbacks, and possible effects on investing strategies that should be considered. Investors should carefully consider their risk tolerance, financial ambitions, and project requirements to choose the best financing option that meets their investment goals. Investors can improve their capacity to take advantage of real estate opportunities, generate sustainable returns, and assemble a broad investment portfolio in the ever-evolving real estate market by utilizing a variety of financing choices and performing extensive due diligence.

Understanding credit scores and their impact

Credit scores are essential for many elements of personal finance. Still, they are necessary for real estate transactions since they significantly impact loan eligibility, mortgage rates, and total borrowing expenses. A person's creditworthiness is represented numerically by their credit score, determined by their financial conduct and credit history. Both potential homeowners and real estate investors need to understand how credit scores are determined, how important they are in real estate transactions, and how to keep or raise a positive score.

Higher scores indicate a reduced credit risk to lenders. Credit scores typically range from 300 to 850. While other elements are considered when calculating credit ratings, payment history is the most important one. On credit cards, loans, and other debts, timely payments show good money management and raise credit ratings. Another important factor is credit use, or the ratio of outstanding debt to credit limits. Lower utilization rates are preferred by lenders since high balances compared to credit limits can be a sign of financial hardship and hurt credit ratings. Credit score computations also consider the length of credit history, the kinds of credit accounts (credit cards, mortgages, and installment loans), and the most recent credit queries.

Credit scores play a crucial role in real estate transactions as they determine a borrower's eligibility for mortgage loans and impact the terms lenders offer. Credit scores are used by mortgage lenders to determine interest rates and to evaluate the risk of default. Higher credit score borrowers are usually eligible for more advantageous loan conditions and lower interest rates, translating into smaller monthly payments and fewer borrowing expenses. On the other hand, poorer credit ratings can make it harder to get a mortgage or lead to higher interest rates, eventually driving up the cost of homeownership.

Consequently, maintaining a high credit score is necessary to maximize affordability in real estate transactions and gain access to competitive financing choices.

Adherence to proper credit practices and proactive money management are necessary for enhancing or preserving a positive credit score. Paying bills and debts on time is essential because missing payments hurt credit ratings. It is possible to guarantee that payments are made on time each month by setting up automated payments or reminders. Appropriately managing credit card balances can positively impact credit scores by avoiding maxing out cards and maintaining low utilization of credit limits. Additionally, it's a good idea to keep various credit accounts active and refrain from opening many new ones quickly, as these acts can temporarily drop credit scores because they result in more queries and a shorter average account age.

To find errors or fraudulent activity that could lower credit scores, it's critical to check credit reports routinely. Under federal law, consumers can obtain free yearly credit reports from each of the three leading credit agencies (Equifax, Experian, and TransUnion). Reviewing these reports, people can confirm the integrity of reported data, including account balances, payment history, and credit inquiries. It is possible to address inconsistencies and stop unjustified harm to credit scores by swiftly disputing errors with credit bureaus.

Those with poor credit histories or ratings may need to take deliberate measures to establish their creditworthiness to develop or restore credit gradually. This can involve getting a secured credit card, in which the credit limit is protected by a deposit, or gaining access to a trusted family member's credit card account as an authorized user. Small purchases and monthly debt repayment in full assist in building a solid payment history and progressively raise credit ratings. By displaying repayment dependability and broadening credit profiles, managing installment loans—such as student or auto loans—responsibly also helps with credit building.

In conclusion, navigating real estate transactions and accomplishing financial goals require an awareness of credit scores and their implications. Credit scores significantly impact borrowing costs, interest rates, and mortgage eligibility. As a result, they affect affordability and financial results for investors and homeowners. People can improve their credit profiles and increase their chances of getting favorable financing terms by upholding excellent credit practices, such as making on-time payments, using credit responsibly, and routinely checking credit reports. To fulfill dreams of becoming a homeowner and experiencing long-term success in real estate investment ventures, it can be beneficial to devote time and energy to establishing and preserving excellent credit.

How to secure the best mortgage rates

Homebuyers and real estate investors must secure the best mortgage rates to reduce borrowing expenses and optimize affordability. Mortgage rates affect monthly mortgage payments and the total cost of financing a property throughout its lifetime by determining the interest rate applied to a home loan. To navigate the mortgage process efficiently, one must thoroughly understand the elements that determine mortgage rates, tactics for securing competitive rates, and considerations when selecting the appropriate mortgage product.

Several economic factors impact mortgage rates, but the Federal Reserve's overall interest rate environment is the main driver. The Federal Reserve's monetary policy choices directly impact short-term interest rates, which also indirectly affect long-term mortgage rates. These decisions include adjustments to the federal funds rate. Economic factors, including inflation, unemployment, and economic development, influence mortgage rates and market expectations. Mortgage rates may increase when the economy is strong, and inflation is low because lenders must respond to increased borrowing costs. In contrast, mortgage rates typically decrease due to lower borrowing costs during recessions or low inflation.

An important consideration in setting the mortgage rates that are made available to borrowers is creditworthiness. Lenders look at several factors to determine a borrower's ability to repay a loan, including debt-to-income ratios, employment histories, credit scores, and stable income. Higher credit scores often translate into better loan conditions and interest rates for borrowers since they are seen as less likely to default. Keeping up a solid credit history by managing your money wisely, paying your bills on time, and avoiding too much debt might help you qualify for more favorable mortgage terms. Before applying for a mortgage, borrowers should examine their credit reports regularly, make any necessary corrections, and take proactive measures to increase their trustworthiness.

Down payments also impact lender-offered mortgage rates and conditions. A higher down payment lowers the loan-to-value ratio (LTV), lessening the lender's risk and making borrowers eligible for cheaper interest rates. To avoid private mortgage insurance (PMI), which raises monthly payments, conventional mortgages frequently need a down payment of at least 20%. Lower down payment choices are available with government-backed loans, such as Federal Housing Administration (FHA) and Veterans Affairs (VA), although they may come with extra fees or insurance premiums. Selecting a suitable down payment amount according to one's mortgage objectives and financial situation might affect the affordability and total cost of borrowing.

Selecting the appropriate mortgage product type is essential to obtaining competitive rates customized to each borrower's financial position and long-term goals. Fixed-rate mortgages provide predictability and security against future rate hikes with consistent monthly payments and interest rates that don't change throughout the loan. After an initial fixed-rate term, adjustable-rate mortgages (ARMs) offer lower interest rates at first and monthly payments that fluctuate based on the state of the market. ARMs can increase long-term costs if interest rates rise sharply and can benefit borrowers who intend to sell or refinance before rate adjustments occur.

By comparing mortgage offers from various lenders, borrowers can determine which financing option is most economical by examining multiple interest rates, fees, and conditions. Lenders may differ in their mortgage rates and closing charges according to their pricing strategies, risk tolerance, and business models. By submitting financial data for evaluation, borrowers can obtain pre-approval from lenders and acquire a conditional commitment for a mortgage amount and interest rate. Pre-approval fortifies negotiation positions during home-buying and shows sellers that you are financially prepared.

Possible benefits of negotiating with lenders include cheaper mortgage rates and closing fees. To obtain better terms, such as lower interest rates or waived fees, borrowers might take advantage of competing offers from several lenders. It is also possible to negotiate points, or up-front payments made to lenders in return for lower interest rates, to lower borrowing expenses throughout the loan. Making educated decisions requires knowing how points affect the overall cost of the loan and figuring out when interest savings will break even to recover upfront expenditures.

Getting the most excellent mortgage rates depends on when you time the market. Borrowers might find advantageous moments to lock in rates before future hikes by examining economic indicators and patterns in interest rates. Mortgage rate locks shield consumers against changes in interest rates while the loan is being processed, which usually takes 30 to 60 days. Rate lock extensions could be offered in case of unforeseen delays or lengthier loan processing timelines. When choosing the best time to lock in mortgage rates, borrowers should consider the market and prospective rate lock costs.

Financial soundness and preparedness for documents are essential to secure competitive rates and speed up the mortgage approval procedure. Lenders look at employment history, asset documentation, income verification, and debt obligations to determine a borrower's credentials and loan eligibility. It is possible to expedite approvals and enable timely rate locking by supplying complete and correct financial information, reacting quickly to lender requests, and keeping lines of communication open throughout the loan process. Consulting with seasoned mortgage consultants and professionals can offer helpful direction on figuring out complicated mortgage products, comprehending different interest rate possibilities, and maximizing borrowing plans customized to each borrower's financial objectives.

Finally, to get the best mortgage rates, one must comprehend economic factors, improve creditworthiness, assess options for a down payment, select suitable mortgage products, compare offers from various lenders, negotiate terms, strategically time rate locks, and maintain financial preparedness throughout the loan process. Through these tactics and expert advice, borrowers can maximize their capacity to get favorable financing alternatives, reduce their borrowing expenses, and attain sustained affordability in their real estate investment and homeownership pursuits.

Creative financing strategies

In the realm of real estate, creative financing strategies refer to novel methods of financing ventures and property purchases that go beyond standard mortgage loans and conventional financing choices. These strategies use complex financial arrangements, alternative capital sources, and negotiation techniques to streamline transactions, optimize investment returns, and get around funding obstacles. Knowing and utilizing innovative financing strategies can provide flexibility, diversification, and increased profitability in real estate endeavors.

Seller financing is a unique approach in which the seller of the property serves as the lender and finances all or part of the purchase price. With the help of this arrangement, purchasers can purchase homes without the need for conventional bank loans, frequently on more accommodating terms arranged directly with the seller. Sellers who want to speed up transactions, make interest income, or postpone paying capital gains taxes in installments may find seller financing appealing. Lower closing costs, quicker transaction times, and the chance to purchase real estate in competitive markets or with limited financing are all advantages for buyers. To match seller financing with investment objectives and financial capacity, it is essential to negotiate advantageous terms, such as interest rates, payback plans, and possible balloon payments.

Rent-to-own contracts and lease alternatives are innovative financing techniques that provide buyers and sellers with flexibility. A lease option gives the buyer the right to lease the property with the option to buy it at a specific price after a predetermined amount of time, usually one to three years. Tenants are given time to raise their credit ratings, save money for a down payment, or assess the property's suitability before deciding to buy, thanks to the option fee and a portion of their monthly rent payments that may be applied toward the purchase price. Reduced vacancy risks, potential property appreciation, and rental income are all advantages for sellers. Similar in operation, rent-to-own contracts usually require tenants to buy the property at the end of the lease period, regardless of the state of the market, giving sellers more security and buyers a planned route to homeownership.

Through Internet platforms, crowdfunding has become a popular creative financing approach that allows various investors to combine their capital to finance real estate projects or purchases. Equity crowdfunding allows investors to purchase ownership holdings in real estate and split appreciation or rental income, with returns given according to the amount invested. With debt crowdfunding, real estate-backed loans are made by investors, who can receive profit-sharing or fixed interest rates in exchange. Real estate investments with various investment sizes, geographic diversification, and the possibility of passive income are all accessible through crowdfunding platforms. Investors should conduct due diligence on project sponsors, property assessments, and platform laws to reduce risks and match financial goals with investments.

Collaborative financing structures such as private equity partnerships and syndications enable investors to pool resources to acquire and manage more significant real estate properties or portfolios. Limited partners give capital and a portion of investment returns, while general partners, usually seasoned real estate experts or investment firms, supervise property purchase, management, and value enhancement initiatives. Through syndications, investors can diversify their holdings, gain access to institutional-quality properties, and benefit from specialized knowledge without burdening to manage real estate themselves. Partnership agreements specify profit-sharing arrangements, governance rights, and departure tactics to guarantee openness, interest alignment, and investor protection. Before investing cash in private equity partnerships or syndications, investors must assess the track records, investment methods, and potential dangers of sponsorships.

Leveraging retirement money or self-directed Individual Retirement Accounts (IRAs) to invest in real estate is another creative financing strategy. Account holders with self-directed IRAs can allocate funds to alternative assets such as real estate partnerships, mortgage notes, and residential and commercial real estate. By leveraging their retirement assets, investors can diversify their holdings, generate tax-deferred or tax-free gains, and match real estate investments to their retirement savings objectives. Self-directed IRA custodians or administrators oversee transactions, make sure rules are followed by the IRS, and offer advice on what investments are permitted and what are not. Investors should confer with tax consultants and legal specialists to optimize investment gains within self-directed IRA designs, handle regulatory intricacies, and comprehend any tax ramifications.

Hard money and bridge loans are short-term financing options that expedite real estate deals by filling funding gaps or enabling speedy acquisitions. Bridge loans offer short-term funding until more long-term funding, such as a conventional mortgage or refinancing, is obtained. Because bridge financing entails more risk and quicker funding schedules, these loans usually have higher interest rates and shorter repayment durations. Hard money loans are asset-based loans that the real estate secures, and lending choices are made primarily on the property's market value rather than the borrower's creditworthiness. Hard money lenders offer flexibility and swift capital deployment; they specialize in providing cash for fix-and-flip projects, renovations, or properties in harmful conditions. Investors should thoroughly review interest rates, loan conditions, and exit plans to control expenses and reduce risks related to bridge and hard money loans.

To sum up, beyond typical mortgage loans and conventional financing methods, creative financing options in real estate offer novel alternatives to finance acquisitions, growing investment portfolios, and improving financial returns. To meet investment goals, take advantage of market opportunities, and overcome obstacles in ever-changing real estate markets, investors can customize financing structures by utilizing seller financing, lease options, crowdfunding, private equity partnerships, self-directed IRAs, bridge loans, and hard money loans. For long-term real estate investing success, maximizing investment potential, minimizing risks, and collaborating with financial advisors are necessary when implementing innovative financing options.

CHAPTER IV

The Purchase Process

Steps to buying a rental property

Purchasing a rental property offers the possibility of long-term appreciation, passive income, and portfolio diversity in the real estate market, making it a potentially profitable investment. A rental property acquisition takes meticulous planning, financial preparation, market research, and strategic decision-making. This book provides essential steps to assist investors in successfully navigating the rental property acquisition process.

Specify the investment criteria and goals. Establishing precise investing objectives and standards is the first stage in purchasing a rental property. Investors ought to ascertain their financial goals, including but not limited to producing rental income, attaining capital growth, and broadening their investment holdings. Defining parameters such as property type (commercial, single-family, or multi-family building), preferred location, financial limits, and projected return on investment (ROI) aids in the process of reducing the number of properties available. It ensures that investment choices align with long-term objectives.

Carry Out Market Analysis. To determine viable investment prospects and evaluate the local real estate market situation, in-depth market research is necessary. The dynamics of supply and demand, vacancy rates, rental patterns, property values, and economic indicators in target markets should all be examined by investors. Job growth, population demographics, infrastructural development, and local amenities influence property demand and rental income potential. Using local market reports, online real estate platforms, and real estate professional networking can yield insightful information that helps with well-informed decision-making.

Safety deposits, getting pre-approval from lenders, investigating mortgage possibilities, and evaluating one's financial preparedness are all necessary steps in obtaining finance for purchasing a rental property. Reviewing their credit history, debt-to-income ratio, and available cash for a down payment and closing costs is suitable for investors. To decide on loan approval and interest rates, mortgage lenders consider borrowers' creditworthiness, income stability, and property eligibility requirements. Finding reasonable financing conditions that complement investment goals and optimize affordability over the loan term is made more accessible by comparing mortgage offers from several lenders.

Determine Adequate Properties. Investors can start finding and assessing possible rental properties that fit their investment criteria as soon as funding is obtained. A few methods for searching for a property include looking through Internet listings, collaborating with real estate brokers specializing in investment properties, going to property auctions, and using networking to find off-market options. Investment decisions are informed and properties are ensured to correspond with investment goals by evaluating property attributes such as condition, location, potential for rental revenue, property management requirements, and expected maintenance expenses.

Exercise Cautious Care. Before finalizing purchase agreements, it is imperative to conduct complete due diligence to evaluate the financial, legal, and physical conditions of potential rental properties. To find any problems or potential liabilities, investors should examine property inspections, appraisals, title records, and property tax assessments. Rent stability and management needs can be ascertained by analyzing rental histories, occupancy rates, leases, and tenant profiles. Using licensed experts, such as property managers, inspectors, and real estate lawyers, can reduce risks and guarantee a thorough assessment of investment possibilities.

Convey Purchase Conditions. To achieve agreements on the acquisition price, financing contingencies, closing dates, and seller concessions that align with investment objectives and market conditions, negotiations are required. Investors can address inspection results, define who is responsible for property transfer and closing fees, and negotiate upgrades or repairs as part of the purchase agreement. Gaining favorable purchase terms and strengthening investors' bargaining power can be achieved by negotiating from a position of knowledge and understanding of the local real estate market and property valuations.

Obtain Financing for Real Estate and Close. Investors proceed with securing property finance and getting ready for closing once they have concluded purchase negotiations and received lender approval. Mortgage lenders work with escrow agents or title companies to organize closing, complete loan underwriting, and confirm property valuations. Investors check loan agreements, insurance policies, settlement statements, and property title transfers for accuracy and contractual compliance before closing on these documents. Upon the completion of loan signings and money transfers, legal possession and property ownership are transferred, officially indicating the rental property's acquisition.

Put Property Management Techniques into Practice. Using efficient property management techniques after purchase is essential to maximizing rental income, preserving property value, and guaranteeing tenant happiness. Investors can choose to handle tenant selection, lease negotiations, rent collection, maintenance requests, and property inspections in-house or by hiring a professional property management company. Positive tenant relations and increased property profitability are fostered by creating clear communication routes with tenants, upholding lease terms, and quickly attending to maintenance needs.

Track and Enhance the Performance of Investments. Rent collection, operational costs, and total property cash flow must all be routinely compared to the initial investment predictions to monitor and optimize investment performance. To find chances for rent hikes, cost-cutting strategies, and property improvements that improve asset value and return on investment, investors monitor rental market changes, vacant properties, and maintenance expenses. Tax methods to maximize returns and reduce taxable income linked with rental property ownership include depreciation deductions and property-related expenses.

Make a plan for long-term expansion and exit tactics. Developing exit and long-term growth plans is critical to optimizing investment returns and adjusting to changing market conditions. Investors can consider using equity from their properties to finance further investments, refinancing to get lower mortgage rates, or diversifying their holdings by selling or exchanging properties. To manage rental property assets for long-term wealth creation, resilience and strategic flexibility are ensured by creating backup plans for unforeseen vacancies, economic downturns, or variations in the real estate market.

To sum up, to take advantage of investment opportunities and meet long-term financial goals in the cutthroat real estate market, purchasing a rental property requires systematic planning, careful research, financial preparedness, and strategic decision-making. Investors can successfully acquire rental properties, maximize investment performance, and create a portfolio of income-producing assets suited to their risk tolerance and financial objectives by following these procedures and utilizing professional experience.

Working with real estate agents and brokers

Interacting with agents and brokers is a crucial step for people navigating the intricacies of purchasing or selling property in the real estate market. To enable successful real estate transactions, these experts offer invaluable knowledge, market insights, negotiating prowess, and transaction management skills. To maximize results and accomplish intended real estate goals, it is crucial to comprehend the roles, advantages, factors, and practical methods for working with real estate agents and brokers.

Licensed professionals representing buyers, sellers, or both in real estate transactions are known as agents and brokers. Agents guide clients through the purchasing or selling process, provide market analysis, appraise properties, and facilitate negotiations while working under the supervision of brokers. In addition to managing their own real estate companies or offices and holding extra certificates, brokers can also provide sophisticated legal or transactional skills, supervise agents' conduct, and ensure regulatory compliance. In real estate transactions, brokers and agents uphold the ethical standards set out by professional associations, state licensing bodies, and client interests. These standards prioritize confidentiality, fiduciary duties, and client interests.

Buyers and sellers can benefit significantly from collaborating with agents and brokers when navigating competitive real estate markets. Agents find properties that match client tastes and investment goals by utilizing their industry connections, local market expertise, and access to extensive listing databases. To increase property visibility and attract qualified purchasers, brokers use strategic marketing strategies for sellers, such as expert photography, property staging, and focused advertising campaigns. The proficiency of agents in property appraisal, bargaining techniques, and contract administration helps buyers make well-informed choices and get the best possible conditions. Along with streamlining the transaction lifecycle, real estate specialists help arrange for appraisals, inspections, and closings. They also advise on financing choices, legal requirements, and potential problems.

Choosing the best real estate broker or agent requires assessing credentials, expertise, and fit with personal tastes and needs. Considerations include the agents' experience in the market, their history of closing deals successfully, their client testimonials, and their familiarity with particular neighborhoods or property types. Online reviews, in-person recommendations, and conversations with potential agents are valuable tools for evaluating an agent's attentiveness, communication style, and dedication to customer pleasure. Clients should confirm the license status of agents, their membership in respectable real estate associations, and their continuous professional development to guarantee adherence to industry norms and expertise in contemporary market trends.

Clear communication and shared expectations are essential for working effectively with brokers and agents in the real estate industry. To effectively direct an agent's search and selection of properties, clients should clearly describe their real estate objectives, timeframe, financial limits, and preferences for particular property features or amenities. To expedite the search process and rank realistic possibilities, agents perform thorough needs assessments, offer market insights, and customize property suggestions per the client's requirements. Open communication and frequent updates on market trends, property showings, and transaction status promote openness, trust, and well-informed decision-making throughout the purchasing or selling process.

Real estate brokers are essential in negotiating purchase offers, counteroffers, and contract terms to get the best results for their clients. Agents formulate competitive bids that match client goals and financial capabilities by utilizing similar property data, market analysis, and insights into seller motivations. Agents handle several offers on sellers' behalf, evaluate buyers' qualifications, and work out terms that will optimize the sale price and reduce contingencies. Agents represent the interests of their clients and help purchasers navigate inspection results, appraisal conclusions, and financing contingencies. They also help buyers resolve transaction issues promptly. To speed up closing procedures and guarantee seamless property transfers, agents ensure that contracts are followed, keep an eye on important deadlines, and arrange to exchange papers between parties.

Real estate agents constantly modify their approaches and use technology breakthroughs to stay ahead of changing market conditions and new trends. Using social media campaigns, virtual tours, and digital marketing platforms, agents may reach a wider audience and connect with tech-savvy buyers and sellers. To foresee changes in the market, spot investment possibilities, and enhance pricing strategies for client listings, brokers use data analytics, predictive modeling, and market forecasting technologies. To stay up to date on regulatory changes, industry best practices, and cutting-edge technology that improves service delivery and customer happiness, real estate professionals engage in continual education and training programs.

Collaborating with competent and seasoned real estate brokers and agents enables people to successfully negotiate the challenges of purchasing or selling real estate with assurance, effectiveness, and positive results. By utilizing professional expertise, market insights, and strategic negotiation abilities, customers can easily attain their specific real estate objectives, making educated decisions and receiving individualized counsel. Whether buying a first home, building investment portfolios, or offloading properties to maximize profits, working with reputable real estate agents guarantees all-encompassing assistance, proactive representation, and the accomplishment of long-term real estate goals in competitive and dynamic marketplaces.

Conducting due diligence (inspections, appraisals, etc.)

When purchasing or investing in real estate, due diligence is an essential step that includes thorough assessments, inspections, appraisals, and evaluations to reduce risks, confirm property value, and guarantee well-informed decision-making. This stage provides information on the property's conditions, legal status, financial viability, and regulatory compliance, protecting buyers, investors, and lenders. Understanding the essential elements and tactical factors of due diligence makes it easier to conduct in-depth property assessments and boosts trust in real estate deals.

Property inspections, which certified inspectors conduct to evaluate a property's operating systems, structural integrity, and physical state, are essential to due diligence. Inspectors assess electrical systems, plumbing, HVAC (heating, ventilation, and air conditioning), roofing, foundation, and other crucial components to find current flaws, safety risks, and required repairs or replacements.

Potential maintenance problems, renovation expenditures, and anticipated lifetime expenses that affect property value and investment returns are all provided to buyers and investors with helpful information. Financial responsibility and transparency in real estate transactions are ensured by addressing inspection findings through agreements for repair credits or price modifications with sellers.

Environmental assessments are carried out, especially for commercial real estate or properties situated in environmentally sensitive locations, to examine potential environmental hazards and liabilities associated with a property. To determine the risks of contamination from hazardous products, pollutants, or nearby properties in the past or present, phase I environmental assessments entail analyzing historical data, conducting site inspections, and conducting interviews. In Phase II evaluations, regulatory compliance and ecological concern mitigation may be achieved by soil testing, groundwater sampling, and remediation planning. To limit legal risk, obtain finance approvals, and put risk management plans into place that safeguard long-term property value and operational viability, lenders and investors evaluate environmental liabilities.

Property appraisals are crucial parts of due diligence to ascertain fair market value and evaluate a property's worth about current market conditions, comparable sales, and investment prospects. To determine precise assessments, licensed appraisers do in-depth evaluations of the property's location, size, condition, features, and current sales data. Appraisals offer unbiased assessment of property values to buyers, sellers, and lenders, assisting in developing well-informed price plans, stances during negotiations, and financing choices. Appraisers adhere to industry standards, regulatory rules, and valuation procedures to assure credibility and dependability in calculating property market values that fit transaction objectives and stakeholder expectations.

Examining property financial statements, income statements, expense reports, and operational records is part of financial due diligence, which assesses the performance of investments, future revenue, and profitability. Investors examine rental income, occupancy rates, lease agreements, and operating expenses to evaluate cash flow stability, return on investment (ROI), and property management efficiency. Through financial due diligence, stakeholders can maximize investment returns and reduce financial risks related to property ownership by identifying revenue sources, cost-saving opportunities, and value-enhancing measures.

Legal due diligence includes examining property titles, deed restrictions, zoning regulations, and legal encumbrances to confirm ownership rights, property boundaries, and compliance with local rules. Real estate attorneys check titles to determine whether liens, easements, or legal conflicts could impact property ownership or future development plans. Clear title and conformity with the law are essential to obtain finance approvals, facilitate property transfers, and prevent legal challenges that could impede transactions or compromise investment outcomes. During due diligence, investors hire attorneys to evaluate contract provisions, arrange contingencies, and guarantee complete legal safeguards.

Market analysis and feasibility studies examine market dynamics, supply and demand trends, demographic profiles, and economic indicators to determine an investment's viability and a property's prospective performance. Investors undertake competitive analysis, property-specific assessments, and demographic research to determine target demographics, rental market trends, and competitive advantages that affect rental income estimates and occupancy rates. To ascertain project feasibility, financial viability, and return on investment (ROI) criteria, feasibility studies assess these factors.

During the property acquisition process, risk management and contingency planning entail identifying potential risks, creating mitigation techniques, and creating backup plans in case something unexpected comes up. To apply risk management techniques that safeguard investment capital, improve property resilience, and maximize investment returns, stakeholders evaluate property risks, financial uncertainties, and market swings. Creating plans to reduce risk, getting insurance, and setting up emergency funds help to reduce the dangers of owning real estate, volatile markets, and business interruptions.

The process of doing due diligence is extensive and includes market studies, evaluations, environmental assessments, financial analyses, legal reviews, and risk management plans. In real estate transactions, thorough due diligence improves transparency, reduces risks, and helps buyers, investors, and lenders make well-informed decisions. Stakeholders can successfully negotiate property acquisitions, optimize investment outcomes, and achieve long-term success in real estate invest.

Closing the deal

In real estate, closing the deal is the last phase, where careful preparation, negotiating, and following the law come together to finish real estate transactions. The efforts of buyers, sellers, real estate brokers, lawyers, and other process participants come to a head at this crucial juncture. Comprehending the complexities, procedures, and factors associated with real estate transaction closure guarantees seamless transfers and favorable results for all stakeholders.

Buyers and sellers complete financial agreements and prepare the paperwork needed to make property transfers easier as the closing date draws near. To ensure funds are available for closing, buyers finalize loan approvals, review loan terms, and work with lenders to get mortgage financing. To complete a legal conveyance, sellers prepare settlement statements, property title paperwork, and any required disclosures. To ensure compliance with contractual commitments and regulatory requirements, real estate professionals—such as attorneys, escrow agents, or title companies—manage document preparations, check transactional details, and mediate communication between parties.

Closing disclosures are provided to buyers before closing, which list the finalized loan terms, itemized closing fees, and financial commitments related to property acquisitions. Closing disclosures, required by the Real Estate Settlement Procedures Act (RESPA) and the Truth in Lending Act (TILA), offer openness regarding escrow account information, loan estimates, and possible revisions to closing expenses based on final calculations. Settlement documents that list transactional costs, credits, and prorated adjustments for buyer-seller reconciliation are reviewed by sellers. These statements include the HUD-1 Settlement Statement and the Closing Disclosure (CD). Before completing legal commitments and property transfers, reviewing closing paperwork assures correctness, adherence to contractual conditions, and mutual knowledge of financial duties.

To confirm property ownership rights, find legal encumbrances, and guarantee clean title transfers at closing, it is essential to conduct a title search. Comprehensive title searches are carried out by title companies or real estate attorneys, who also examine public records, property liens, easements, and restrictions that can impact ownership rights or property transactions. Title insurance policies offer financial protection against potential losses or legal obligations by shielding buyers and lenders from unforeseen title flaws, claims, or disputes that arise after property transfers. Before completing closing deals, buyers and sellers check title insurance obligations, settle title disputes, and accept final title policies to guarantee secure property ownership and legal protections.

To start the closing process, buyers and sellers study and sign legal documents, such as mortgage notes, deeds of trust, property disclosures, and settlement statements. To ensure compliance with state laws, contractual duties, and industry standards for property transfers, real estate attorneys or escrow agents supervise the signing of documents. Acknowledging the mortgage commitments, repayment terms, and regulatory disclosures stated in loan agreements, buyers sign loan documents. Under the terms and conditions, sellers execute property deeds, giving buyers legal ownership rights and transferring property titles. In closing, document signatures confirm transactional promises, guarantee property transfer, and create legal frameworks that safeguard the interests of the buyer and seller and guarantee legally binding contracts.

Fund disbursements are managed by escrow agents or title companies, who help with payments for closing costs, seller proceeds, property purchases, and loan payoffs. Buyers supply certified money or wire transfers to pay for down payments, closing charges, and other pre-paid expenses related to purchasing real estate. Sellers get the proceeds from selling their properties after deducting mortgage payments, unpaid liens, and closing costs. To complete ownership transfers and legal conveyances, escrow agents disburse money to creditors, pay off current mortgages or liens, and register property deeds with county or local authorities. Successful closing transactions result from completing fund disbursements and property transfers, guaranteeing financial settlements, removing title encumbrances, and creating new ownership rights.

Buyers take ownership obligations after property closings, initiate insurance coverage, and arrange utility transfers to ensure smooth transitions and occupation. By the terms of the contract, sellers depart premises, schedule final property inspections or repairs, and give buyers or property managers access codes, keys, and significant property details. Real estate agents handle concerns walkthrough properties and ensure contingencies and contractual duties are followed to streamline post-closing interactions, handle transactional issues, and uphold client relationships. After a successful closing, sellers finish relocation plans, money settlements, and future real estate plans while buyers celebrate new property purchases, furnish living areas, and begin homeownership journeys.

To achieve successful outcomes, closing a real estate deal requires careful planning, practical discussions, and cooperative efforts by buyers, sellers, and real estate experts. Achieving smooth property transfers, reducing transactional risks, and upholding ethical standards in real estate activities are all made possible by stakeholders who manage closing procedures, finalize financial arrangements, examine legal papers, and comply with regulatory regulations. In real estate transactions, all parties benefit from improved confidence, trust, and pleasure from effective communication, transparency, and adherence to closing timeframes. This creates favorable experiences and long-lasting partnerships in competitive and dynamic markets.

CHAPTER V

Renovations and Property Improvements

Assessing necessary renovations and improvements

In real estate investing and property management, determining what renovations and improvements are required to maximize property value, draw in tenants, and guarantee long-term profitability is an essential first step. Achieving intended results and maximizing return on investment (ROI) requires careful assessments and strategic planning for repairs and enhancements, whether buying a new property or reviving an existing investment. Investors, property owners, and managers can make well-informed judgments and navigate renovation projects in competitive real estate markets by solidly understanding the critical factors, renovation tactics, and cost-effective upgrades.

A thorough needs assessment and an initial inspection of the property are the first steps in determining necessary repairs. Upon site inspections, investors and property managers assess the operational systems, structural integrity, and physical conditions to find possible flaws, safety risks, and areas for improvement. To establish maintenance needs, repair priorities, and the viability of renovations, assessments include examining the interior finishes, roofing, HVAC (heating, ventilation, and air conditioning) systems, plumbing, electrical, and flooring systems. Prioritizing and allocating funds for rehabilitation projects are guided by determining which areas require immediate attention against long-term improvement goals. This ensures that the projects align with property investment goals and market demands.

Determining remodeling techniques that optimize the attractiveness of a property and its rental potential requires thorough market study and a grasp of tenant preferences. Investors examine local market trends, demographic profiles, and competitive rental properties to determine tenant demographics, lifestyle choices, and amenity preferences that influence rental demand and occupancy rates. To meet the expectations of both tenants and the market, renovation decisions are informed by market insights. Examples of these decisions include modernizing bathroom fixtures, replacing kitchen appliances, and improving outdoor living spaces. Renovations tailored to the market's needs increase a property's value, draw in desirable tenants, and enable competitive rental pricing methods that maximize long-term property appreciation and rental income.

To achieve the best return on investment, cost-effective renovation techniques must balance desired upgrades and budgetary restrictions. Improvements that improve curb appeal with landscaping, paint exteriors, or install energy-efficient windows and doors to increase property aesthetics and energy efficiency are improvements that investors prioritize because they give the highest returns on investment. Upgrades to the kitchen and bathrooms are the main emphasis of interior renovations; to improve utility, aesthetic appeal, and tenant happiness, old worktops, cabinets, and fixtures are replaced. Replacing flooring, painting walls, and adding contemporary lighting fixtures all help create hospitable living areas that draw in potential renters and enable greater rental yields in cutthroat rental markets.

Renovating a property with energy-efficient and sustainable modifications encourages environmental stewardship, lowers operating costs, and increases marketability. Energy-efficient appliances, LED lighting fixtures, and programmable thermostats are top priorities for investors to reduce utility costs, draw in environmentally concerned renters, and adhere to building laws and standards for energy efficiency. Enhancing resource conservation, promoting sustainable living habits, and attracting ecologically conscious renters looking for eco-friendly rental options are all made possible by installing low-flow plumbing fixtures, water-saving toilets, and effective HVAC systems. Renovating a property sustainably helps buildings stand out in competitive rental markets and positions investments for long-term profitability and tenant retention.

During the design and execution of remodeling projects, ensuring compliance with local building standards, zoning restrictions, and permit requirements is crucial. To secure required licenses, conduct inspections, and comply with regulatory norms governing property upgrades, investors work with licensed contractors, architects, and building inspectors. Adherence to safety protocols, rules for accessibility, and environmental regulations serve to reduce legal risks, avert expensive penalties, and safeguard real estate investments against possible liabilities that may arise from non-compliance. To maintain industry standards and foster positive relationships with regulatory bodies, community stakeholders, and tenants, property owners and managers prioritize openness, accountability, and ethical procedures when undertaking restoration projects.

Properly completing property upgrades, cost control, and minimal disruptions depend on efficient project management and deadline adherence. During renovation, investors set project goals, budgetary restrictions, and performance standards to track progress, manage resources effectively, and handle unforeseen issues. Renovation projects are completed on schedule, under budget, and with quality control thanks to the involvement of qualified contractors, supervision of subcontractors, and upkeep of open lines of communication. To track project milestones, keep an eye on spending, and assess ROI criteria that gauge the effects of renovations on property value and rental income production, investors use project management tools, software programs, and performance indicators.

Evaluating the state of a property, comprehending market dynamics, and putting cost-effective methods into practice are all part of the strategic process of determining what upgrades and changes are essential to boost the property's value and rental appeal. In competitive real estate markets, investors and property owners can maximize returns on investment, draw in quality tenants, and maintain long-term profitability by conducting in-depth property evaluations, prioritizing tenant preferences, incorporating sustainable upgrades, guaranteeing regulatory compliance, and effectively managing renovation projects. In real estate investment activities that aim to achieve superior asset performance and stakeholder satisfaction, resilience, growth, and success are fostered by strategic planning, proactive decision-making, and commitment to property enhancement projects.

Budgeting for renovations

Achieving desired results within predetermined budgetary restrictions requires careful financial planning, cost analysis, and intelligent resource allocation. These are crucial components of a successful real estate investment and property management budget for renovations. Whether remodeling a home, business, or investment property, knowing critical budgetary criteria, cost variables, and practical tactics guarantees responsible money management, optimizes return on investment (ROI), and raises the property's value. To maximize asset performance and attain long-term profitability in volatile real estate markets, investors, property owners, and managers handle restoration projects with vision, openness, and strict budgeting procedures.

To ascertain the project's scope, scale, and related costs, an initial cost estimate and thorough needs assessment are conducted before beginning the budgeting process for renovations. Property managers and investors evaluate the state of the properties, determine which renovations should be prioritized, and rank the areas of improvement according to market demand, functional upgrades, and aesthetic enhancements. Needs evaluations include assessing the mechanical systems, interior finishes, and structural integrity to address building code compliance, maintenance difficulties, and safety concerns. Working with licensed architects, contractors, or property inspectors makes it easier to predict costs accurately, evaluate viability, and develop affordable restoration plans that respect financial limits and investment objectives.

Developing a comprehensive renovation budget entails breaking down project costs and assigning money for supplies, labor, permits, and emergency savings to reduce financial risk and unanticipated project charges. Investors incorporate cost breakdowns for interior finishes, plumbing, electrical, and demolition work into budget spreadsheets or financial management systems to properly track expenses, monitor cash flow, and manage project timetables. Through establishing cost controls, performance indicators, and budgetary benchmarks, stakeholders may assess the viability of projects, rank potential investments, and allocate resources optimally for upgrades that optimize property value and tenant satisfaction.

Renovating projects within budgetary constraints and attaining desired investment returns requires careful consideration of cost considerations and strategic budgetary resource allocation. Labor rates, material costs, travel charges, and administrative fees related to renovation activities are some cost variables. Investors bargain for competitive bids, request estimates from several contractors, and take advantage of bulk purchasing discounts to lower procurement costs without sacrificing project timeliness or quality. Setting aside money for essential renovations like roof replacements, HVAC upgrades, and structural repairs first assures property durability, tenant satisfaction, and regulatory compliance, improving asset resilience and marketability in highly competitive real estate markets.

Renovation budgets that include contingency planning and risk management techniques are protected from unanticipated difficulties, market shifts, and project delays that result in cost overruns and business interruptions. During renovation phases, contingency reserves, which usually range from 10% to 20% of overall project costs, offer financial buffers for unexpected repairs, scope modifications, material shortages, and regulatory compliance difficulties. Investors work with project managers, attorneys, and insurance companies to identify project risks, obtain performance bonds, and put risk mitigation strategies into place that safeguard investment funds, reduce financial obligations, and guarantee adherence to project schedules and quality standards.

Value-enhancing remodeling tactics in competitive real estate markets improve property appreciation, tenant retention, and rental income potential. Renovations that have the highest return on investment (ROI), such as updated kitchens and bathrooms, new flooring, and energy-efficient modifications that satisfy modern tenant wants and preferences, are given priority by investors. Improving curb appeal through exterior painting, landscaping, or eco-friendly features draws potential renters, supports higher rental rates, and enhances the property's overall aesthetics. Value-driven renovations position assets for long-term growth and profitability in real estate portfolios, differentiate buildings in competitive markets, and line with market expectations.

Maintaining renovation budgets, keeping track of project costs, and evaluating ROI metrics—which gauge how renovations affect property value and investment returns—depend on ongoing financial monitoring and performance review. Investors monitor cash flow, reconcile expenses, and examine variance reports that contrast actual spending with budgeted allocations using accounting systems, financial management software, and budget tracking tools. To prioritize capital renovations, increase asset performance across various real estate portfolios, and refine future budgeting methods, performance evaluations analyze renovation outcomes, tenant satisfaction levels, and property marketability.

Strategic planning, thorough cost analysis, and disciplined financial management techniques are necessary for renovation budgeting to maximize investment returns in real estate markets and accomplish desired results. By implementing comprehensive needs assessments, meticulous budgets for renovations, strategic resource allocation, and value-enhancing tactics, investors and property owners can augment property value, draw in high-caliber tenants, and maintain long-term profitability in highly competitive real estate markets. In dynamic and changing real estate markets, proactive budgeting techniques, risk management plans, and ongoing performance reviews guarantee financial transparency, operational effectiveness, and the successful completion of renovation projects that meet stakeholder expectations and investment goals.

DIY vs. hiring professionals

A crucial decision that homeowners, real estate investors, and renovators must make when considering modifying their properties is whether to hire specialists or start DIY house repairs. Every strategy has its benefits and drawbacks, which can be influenced by the project's complexity, the individual's skill level, time commitment, financial limits, and the expected degree of output quality.

DIY renovations appeal to people who enjoy being hands-on and having the chance to customize their living areas to fit their tastes and vision. Homeowners who take on projects independently can fully express their creativity, from choosing materials and design features to renovating at their own speed. Because do-it-yourselfers may buy components at retail prices and save the labor costs associated with employing specialists, this technique frequently results in significant cost savings. When completed with personal craftsmanship and imagination, DIY projects build a deeper connection to the home and provide a sense of satisfaction and success beyond financial considerations.

DIY projects do, however, provide several difficulties and possible disadvantages. While many homeowners can easily do basic renovations like painting walls or adding shelves, more intricate projects like structural alterations, plumbing upgrades, or electrical work call for specific expertise and abilities. DIYers risk making mistakes that could result in expensive repairs, safety risks, or even construction laws and regulations infractions if they need to gain the necessary skills. The time and effort required to finish DIY projects can also be significant, particularly when balancing obligations like job and family.

Hiring specialists adds a degree of knowledge, effectiveness, and quality assurance for home improvements that do-it-yourself projects might only sometimes provide. Professional designers, builders, and contractors have the education, expertise, and credentials to carry out intricate renovations precisely, safely, and by regional building codes. They also provide industry contacts, specialist tools, and an up-to-date understanding of building materials and methods, guaranteeing excellent craftsmanship and long-lasting outcomes.

In addition to their technical expertise, professional services provide efficient project management and subcontractor coordination, which can significantly accelerate remodeling projects and reduce disruptions to everyday life. Contractors are skilled at managing logistical difficulties, obtaining required licenses, and staying within project budgets and schedules. Furthermore, trustworthy contractors frequently guarantee labor and supplies, giving homeowners peace of mind and a safety net if unanticipated problems or flaws appear after repairs.

Professional services have benefits, but they also have costs that should be considered when creating a homeowner's budget. Hiring contractors might result in higher prices than the initial estimates given because of labor fees, overhead, and material markups. To prevent misunderstandings and disagreements, homeowners should consider these costs about the advantages of professional experience and efficiency. They should also ensure contractual agreements, payment schedules, and project deliverables clarity.

DIY projects could be a more cost-effective option for people on a low budget or who prioritize cost control, especially for little repairs or aesthetic enhancements. However, the property's long-term value, durability, and resale potential frequently make the investment in professional services worthwhile when taking on larger-scale restorations or projects requiring technical skills, safety compliance, or structural integrity.

Homeowners frequently find success by implementing hybrid strategies that combine do-it-yourself projects with expert assistance, maximizing the benefits of each strategy while minimizing its drawbacks. With this cooperative approach, homeowners can take on more manageable jobs while hiring experts to handle crucial parts of the restoration project, such as structural repairs, plumbing installs, and electrical rewiring.

Homeowners can maximize project outcomes, increase productivity, and guarantee regulatory compliance by using their DIY skills for activities that are within their capabilities and hiring professionals for specialized labor. Professionals and do-it-yourselfers working together promote information exchange, skill development, and mutual support, which opens up opportunities for learning and development while accomplishing restoration goals.

The choice between doing repairs yourself and hiring specialists ultimately boils down to carefully evaluating each person's abilities, the project needs, available funds, and the desired results. Whereas professional services give knowledge, effectiveness, and a guarantee of quality when carrying out intricate improvements, do-it-yourself projects offer independence, financial savings, and personal fulfillment through participation. Through hybrid methodologies, homeowners can optimize the advantages of expert assistance and do-it-yourself efforts, resulting in successful and fulfilling remodeling experiences that improve the aesthetic appeal, functionality, and overall value of their houses.

Enhancing property value through strategic upgrades

For homeowners, real estate investors, and property managers who want to optimize the appeal, usability, and marketability of residential and commercial properties, strategically upgrading a property is a critical component of their overall plan. In competitive real estate markets, strategic upgrades refer to a set of modifications specifically designed to fulfill the market's needs, improve curb appeal, and increase overall property value. By identifying critical areas for enhancement, prioritizing economic changes, and utilizing market trends, interested parties can maximize their return on investment (ROI) and situate their properties for sustained growth and financial gain.

The first step in increasing the value of a property is to pinpoint essential areas that need to be improved to meet tenant preferences, market expectations, and property-specific features. Both homeowners and investors perform extensive assessments of their properties, evaluating the external and interior features, the structural soundness, and the functional aspects to pinpoint any flaws, out-of-date components, or areas that may be improved. Modernizing fixtures, replacing appliances, and enhancing storage options to improve practicality and visual appeal are all common interior upgrades that concentrate on kitchen and bathroom renovations, which are known to provide excellent returns on investment. Modern flooring materials, energy-efficient windows, and improved lighting fixtures all help create livable areas that appeal to renters and potential buyers looking for contemporary conveniences and comfortable lifestyles.

Cost-effective upgrades should be prioritized by weighing the costs of the investment against the possibility of returns and market value growth. Upgrades that maximize resource management and budget allocation while having the most significant impact on property value are emphasized as strategic upgrades. Improved external landscaping, exterior painting, and installing curb appeal elements like outdoor lighting or paths all improve the property's appearance, raise curb appeal, and produce positive first impressions that draw in prospective tenants or buyers. Putting money into long-lasting materials, fine craftsmanship, and environmentally friendly renovations promotes long-term property upkeep, lowers operating expenses, and increases a property's resistance to changing market conditions.

Market trends and buyer preferences guide innovation decisions that adhere to modern industry standards, design aesthetics, and technological improvements. Renovation plans that target specific audiences and increase the desirability of a property are informed by an understanding of changing consumer habits, lifestyle preferences, and demographic trends. Eco-friendly amenities, energy-efficient appliances, and smart home technology appeal to renters and buyers concerned about the environment and looking for cost-effective ways to live sustainably. In addition to meeting changing lifestyle needs, interior design that allows for multipurpose living areas, home gyms, or flexible work-from-home environments can improve a property's market attractiveness and versatility in cutthroat real estate markets.

Improving a home's curb appeal with well-planned modifications is crucial to making an excellent first impression and drawing in potential tenants or buyers. To enhance external aesthetics and create welcoming settings for outdoor entertaining or relaxation, exterior renovations concentrate on renovating outdoor living spaces like patios, decks, or garden areas and maintaining lawn care. Improving the curb appeal of a property by painting the outside, adding new siding, or changing the roofing materials makes the property look better, resists weather better, and has a higher overall value, making it more desirable to renters or potential buyers who are looking for well-kept, aesthetically pleasing properties.

Implementing strategic renovations that enhance property value, set homes apart from competitors, and appeal to specific market segments is necessary to optimize properties' return on investment and marketability. Enhancing interior finishes with sturdy materials and contemporary design aesthetics, installing energy-efficient HVAC systems, and updating kitchen appliances improve a property's functionality, appeal to potential tenants or buyers, and support competitive rental pricing strategies that maximize long-term property appreciation and rental income potential. In competitive real estate markets, energy-efficient renovations, automated security systems, and smart home technologies boost operational performance, property efficiency, and tenant happiness while lowering maintenance costs and property value.

Strategic upgrades to increase property value entail identifying important improvement areas, prioritizing cost-effective upgrades, and taking advantage of market trends to maximize return on investment and property marketability. In vibrant and competitive real estate markets, homeowners, investors, and property managers can maximize property value, draw in potential tenants or buyers, and achieve long-term profitability and appreciation by concentrating on interior and exterior renovations that improve functionality, aesthetics, and sustainability.

CHAPTER VI

Marketing Your Rental Property

Creating effective rental listings

Attracting suitable renters, increasing occupancy rates, and optimizing rental income depends on your ability to market your property efficiently through eye-catching rental listings. Strategic planning, meticulous attention to detail, and the capacity to draw attention to your property's unique qualities and advantages for potential tenants are all necessary when creating a successful rental listing. Landlords and property managers may design effective rental listings that stand out in competitive rental markets and appeal to target demographics by concentrating on essential components, including property description, picture, price strategy, and distribution channels.

A property description that effectively conveys the qualities of your property and appeals to prospective tenants is the cornerstone of any successful rental listing. Start by emphasizing essential details like the square footage, number of bedrooms and bathrooms, and other features like a backyard, modern kitchen appliances, or easy access to public transportation. Please describe the property's flow and layout, highlighting the unique features that set it apart from other rental options and its practical features. Draw a clear picture of the kind of living that renters might anticipate using descriptive language and emphasizing features like lots of storage space, natural lighting, or contemporary architectural elements that improve comfort and convenience.

To draw in potential tenants and highlight the features of your rental property, you must provide high-quality pictures and graphic content. Get a high-resolution camera or hire a professional photographer to take crisp, well-lit photos of every room, the property's exterior, and its salient features. Emphasizing appealing features like remodeled interiors, beautifully landscaped gardens, or picturesque views strengthens the rental property's value proposition and improves visual appeal. To attract potential tenants and help them picture themselves living there, provide a range of images that give a thorough overview of the property, including common areas, outdoor areas, and distinctive architectural aspects.

Creating a competitive pricing plan based on in-depth market research is essential to draw in renters and increase rental income. To gain insight into current market trends, rental rates, and tenant preferences, research comparable homes for rent in the vicinity. When choosing rental pricing that accurately captures the value your property offers, consider elements like location, size, condition, and the amenities close by. To attract potential renters, you should set your rental price competitively while evaluating the property's unique attributes, market demand, and ability to provide positive cash flow. To learn more about the best pricing tactics that maximize occupancy rates and rental returns, use property management software, online rental price calculators, or advice from real estate experts.

For your rental listing to grab attention and entice potential tenants to learn more, you must create an engaging headline and emphasize important property attributes. Use a clear and descriptive headline highlighting the property's unique features, such as "Charming Family Home Near Top-Rated Schools and Parks" or "Spacious Downtown Apartment with Panoramic City Views." Emphasize benefits like improved appliances, pet-friendly policies, flexible leasing terms, or close access to nearby activities and amenities by highlighting essential characteristics in bullet points or brief paragraphs. A property's highlights should be tailored to your target tenant group's tastes and lifestyle requirements, highlighting features that appeal to tenants looking for particular amenities or ways of living.

To help potential tenants understand the lease terms, rental obligations, and any additional costs related to the property, include clear and informative rental terms in your listing. Describe the length of the lease, the rental application process, the security deposit requirements, and any tenant requirements that may be unique, such as income verification or a minimum credit score. Set expectations and guarantee clarity throughout renting by communicating utility duties, parking arrangements, pet policies, and maintenance procedures in plain language. By providing contact details for questions or arranging property tours, you may encourage potential tenants to proceed and ensure that any issues or queries they may have concerned the rental property are promptly resolved.

Your rental listing will be more visible and reachable and draw on a broader pool of possible tenants if you use efficient distribution methods and promotional tactics. Post rental listings for your property on well-known real estate websites, rental listing services, and social media platforms that tenants in your target market use. Use email marketing, social media campaigns, and internet advertising to advertise your listing and interact with potential tenants. Work with neighborhood relocation agencies, property management firms, and real estate brokers to increase the visibility of your rental and gain access to their pool of potential tenants.

In competitive rental markets, creating great rental listings is essential to marketing your property and drawing in quality tenants. Landlords and property managers may maximize their homes' exposure, attractiveness, and rental success by creating captivating property descriptions, adding top-notch visual content, creating a strategic pricing plan, and leveraging efficient distribution methods. Optimizing rental listings to emphasize salient features, convey unambiguous rental agreements, and interact with potential tenants via focused promotional campaigns improves the rental experience. It boosts occupancy rates, long-term tenant satisfaction, and real estate investment profitability.

Utilizing online platforms and social media

Social media and internet platforms are now essential for individuals, companies, and groups in various sectors, including real estate. Leveraging online platforms and social media channels presents opportunities to improve exposure, interact with potential clients, and spur business growth in real estate marketing and property management. Real estate agents may increase their reach, build relationships, and optimize marketing tactics to promote properties effectively, draw in quality leads, and meet sales or rental goals by utilizing the power of digital tools and social networking sites.

Property listings are displayed to a global audience of prospective buyers or renters through online platforms like real estate websites, property listing portals, and rental marketplaces. These online resources include detailed property information, excellent photos, virtual tours, and interactive maps to help potential buyers make educated decisions and expedite the real estate search. Real estate agents use these platforms to list properties, emphasize salient characteristics, and highlight distinctive selling propositions that set them apart in crowded markets. Agents and property managers can boost their online visibility and draw in quality leads interested in buying or renting homes by refining property descriptions, employing search engine optimization (SEO) strategies, and keeping up-to-date listings.

Real estate professionals have channels through social media platforms like Facebook, Instagram, LinkedIn, and Twitter to engage with various individuals, establish their brands, and cultivate deep connections with industry stakeholders and prospective clients. Social media marketing tactics include producing exciting content, disseminating real estate listings, uploading virtual tours or property videos, and writing educational blog entries or articles that demonstrate subject matter expertise and benefit followers. Real estate professionals can humanize their brand, showcase properties in real-time, and build a community of engaged followers interested in real estate trends, market updates, and property investment opportunities by utilizing visual content, compelling storytelling, and interactive features like live streams or Q&A sessions.

Real estate agents can reach particular demographics, geographic areas, and buyer or renter personas based on their interests, behaviors, and online activities by using internet platforms and social media for customized advertising and retargeting campaigns. Agents can strategically promote property listings, highlight open houses, and create leads by targeting people actively searching for real estate opportunities or exhibiting interest in related topics through paid advertising on platforms such as Google Ads, Facebook Ads, or LinkedIn Ads. Through customized messaging and content, retargeting campaigns connect potential customers who have already looked at property listings or interacted with the agent's website. This increases brand visibility, nurtures leads, and promotes conversion.

Using data analytics and insights obtained from social media analytics tools and online platforms, real estate professionals may monitor user engagement, analyze campaign performance, and optimize marketing tactics based on decisions that can be taken immediately. Agents can find practical marketing approaches, improve targeting methods, and allocate resources efficiently to maximize return on investment (ROI) by evaluating metrics like website traffic, click-through rates, audience demographics, and engagement levels across digital platforms. In competitive real estate markets, data-driven insights guide strategic modifications, content optimizations, and ad spend allocations that improve campaign performance, attract quality traffic, and ease lead generation and conversion.

Creating a professional online presence, providing insightful information, and authentically interacting with customers and prospects are all essential to developing trust and credibility using social media and online platforms. Real estate agents utilize social media channels to exhibit successful transactions, offer client testimonials, and highlight industry expertise through market insights, thought leadership content, and instructional tools. Through active participation in industry discussions, prompt inquiry responses, and transparent property and market information disclosures, agents establish rapport, cultivate trust, and position themselves as reliable advisors who can confidently lead clients through the buying, selling, or renting process in real estate.

Using virtual reality (VR) tours, augmented reality (AR) experiences, 3D modeling, and drone photography to create immersive property experiences that appeal to potential renters or purchasers is all part of embracing virtual technology and innovation in real estate marketing. These technologies improve convenience, accessibility, and engagement for distant clients or foreign investor Engagement in virtual property viewings, interactive floor plans, and thorough property inspections from anywhere in the world. To highlight architectural features, property features, and provide a comprehensive viewing experience that expedites decision-making, reduces the need for in-person visits, and promotes smooth transactions in a cutthroat international market, real estate professionals use virtual tools and digital innovations.

Real estate marketing has been transformed by social media and online platforms, which provide solid tools and digital methods to increase engagement, broaden reach, and spur company growth Engagement at marketplaces. Real estate professionals can enhance property visibility, establish connections with specific audiences, cultivate clientele, and accomplish marketing goals that bolster sustained prosperity, financial gain, and sector leadership by skillfully utilizing these digital platforms in the dynamic domain of real estate investments and property administration.

Staging and photographing your property

The first impressions that prospective tenants or purchasers get of your property can significantly impact their opinion of its worth and livability, so staging and taking photos of it are essential steps in getting your property ready for sale or renting. When a home is staged well, it becomes a warm, inviting area that shows its most excellent qualities, makes the most use of available space, and appeals to the target market. Stagers create an atmosphere that appeals to potential renters or buyers by carefully placing furniture, accessories, and decor to evoke strong feelings and make it easier for people to picture themselves living there.

Decluttering, depersonalizing, and rearranging furniture are all part of home staging, which aims to maximize each room's flow and utility while highlighting the building's architectural details and abundant natural light. Stage managers frequently employ sophisticated design, modern furniture, and neutral color schemes to create a unified, inviting space that appeals to many viewers.

Staging increases the property's appeal, draws attention to its potential, and presents a lifestyle that appeals to purchasers or renters looking for a move-in ready home or investment opportunity. This is accomplished by removing personal belongings, reducing visual distractions, and improving spatial organization.

To create focal points and attract attention, staging skillfully highlights the property's architectural features and unique selling elements, such as built-in bookcases, fireplaces, or panoramic views, showcasing its unique charm and character. Professional stagers arrange furniture in balanced patterns that maximize space and improve each room's apparent size and usability, considering traffic flow, spatial proportions, and functionalities. Staging boosts the property's marketability, increases its perceived worth, and sets it apart from other properties in the marketplace by adding features of elegance, comfort, and functionality.

To effectively sell real estate, photography is essential. It captures the spirit and aesthetic appeal of arranged properties with eye-catching photos that draw attention and pique the interest of potential tenants or buyers both online and in print media. Expert photographers capture appealing angles, highlight salient aspects that increase the property's appeal, and display natural light using cutting-edge camera gear, lighting strategies, and composition concepts. To captivate target audiences, photographs should evoke a feeling of openness, atmosphere, and way of life that compels viewers to go further and see themselves relocating there.

Developing captivating visual narratives that convey information about the home's lifestyle, features, and unique selling points is essential to compelling property photography. To present a complete picture of the property's appeal and potential, photographers take inside and exterior photos highlighting landscaping elements, outdoor facilities, and architectural details. Photographers can add visual appeal, depth, and meaning to their work by combining wide-angle pictures, close-up details, and aerial viewpoints captured with drone photography. This creates an immersive viewing experience that improves viewers' emotional connection and decision-making ability.

Adding interactive media, 3D floor plans, and virtual tours improves the online viewing experience by letting potential tenants or buyers virtually tour the property from the comfort of their homes or mobile devices. With the help of interactive walkthroughs that mimic in-person visits, virtual tours let users explore rooms, enlarge details, and see spatial layouts in real time. Virtual tours enhance user engagement, expand the visibility of a property, and draw in serious queries from prospective tenants or buyers who live far away and value accessibility, ease of use, and clear visual transparency.

To optimize property visibility and draw in a wide range of potential buyers or renters, staging and professional photography support multichannel marketing tactics, such as online property listings, social media platforms, real estate websites, and print advertising. Staged photography is a powerful tool used by real estate agents and marketing specialists to produce eye-catching digital brochures, promotional materials, and marketing collateral that successfully communicates the property's value proposition and highlights its attraction. Marketers can increase property exposure in competitive real estate markets, provide qualified leads, and enable successful property transactions by streamlining distribution methods, focusing on particular demographics, and implementing customized advertising campaigns.

Staging and photographing your property are crucial for effective real estate marketing techniques to improve visual appeal, marketability, and buyer or renter engagement in competitive markets. To enhance the presentation of properties, set themselves apart from competitors, and draw in qualified buyers or tenants looking for investment opportunities or desirable, move-in-ready homes, homeowners, real estate agents, and property managers can invest in professional staging services, use superior photography techniques, and integrate immersive digital media. In addition to improving a property's aesthetics and marketability, successful staging and photography contribute to increased resale values, quicker sales turnover, and satisfied clients—all of which are critical factors in real estate investing and property management's long-term success and profitability.

Setting competitive rental prices

Landlords, property managers, and real estate investors must set competitive rental prices to maximize income potential and draw in qualified tenants in the ever-changing rental market. To obtain competitive rental rates that align with property value and market demand, effective pricing strategies entail a careful balance between market dynamics, property attributes, geographic advantages, and tenant preferences.

Understanding market dynamics and local rental patterns in great detail is the first step in establishing competitive rental prices. Real estate experts perform thorough market research to determine rental rates for similar homes in the same neighborhood or location. They consider several aspects, including property size, condition, amenities, and proximity to commercial centers, transit hubs, and schools. Rent pricing decisions are influenced by supply and demand dynamics, which can be understood through the analysis of vacancy rates, tenant demographics, and economic factors. Landlords can adjust pricing tactics to take advantage of opportunities, reduce risks, and preserve competitive positioning in the rental market by keeping abreast of market swings, seasonal variations, and developing trends.

Setting competitive rental rates that accurately reflect the property's appeal and attraction to potential renters requires analyzing its attributes and figuring out its distinctive value proposition. Higher rental rates are obtained for properties with enhanced facilities, contemporary appliances, energy-efficient features, and luxury finishes as opposed to conventional or outmoded flats. The large layouts, the picturesque views, the outdoor amenities, and the proximity to the cultural or recreational attractions are some of the unique selling points that landlords emphasize to attract the target tenant demographics looking for convenience or a particular lifestyle.

Setting reasonable price expectations that optimize rental revenue potential while remaining competitive and enticing to potential renters is essential to strike a balance between rental income goals and market demand. To establish a sustainable price plan that supports financial objectives and is in line with regional market conditions, landlords compute rental yields based on investment objectives, operational costs, property maintenance costs, and prospective vacancy risks. It could be required to modify prices in response to shifts in the market, tenant demand, or competitive environment to ensure properties remain appealing and competitive in luring and keeping good renters.

Landlords and property managers can more precisely determine the worth of their properties and set rental rates using comparative market analysis (CMA) tools and specialist knowledge. To determine pricing trends, rental trends, and competitive benchmarks that guide pricing decisions, CMAs assess current rental transactions, rental histories, and property performance data. Landlords may optimize property income and occupancy levels by studying CMA data to obtain valuable insights into tenant preferences, rental rate variations, and competitive advantages. These insights can then be utilized to lead strategic pricing adjustments, lease renewals, and tenant retention initiatives.

Using dynamic pricing strategies, property income and occupancy rates are maximized throughout the leasing cycle by adjusting rental rates in response to seasonal demand swings, real-time market data, and tenant behavior. When tenant decision-making and rental affordability are affected by competing developments, local events, economic conditions, or peak leasing seasons, landlords may decide to modify rental costs. To anticipate market trends, spot pricing possibilities, and proactively modify rental rates toto draw in quality tenants and reduce vacancy risks, dynamic pricing techniques use pricing algorithms, rental analytics platforms, and predictive modeling tools.

Setting competitive rental pricing that supports rental rates and set houses apart in the market requires promoting value and improving property appeal. To enhance curb appeal, interior aesthetics, and overall tenant satisfaction, landlords make aesthetic modifications, upgrades, and maintenance investments in their properties. Through virtual tours, professional photography, and compelling property descriptions, landlords can effectively showcase their properties' features, amenities, and lifestyle benefits. This approach helps them create a compelling value proposition that appeals to potential tenants and supports competitive rental rates that align with the property quality, location advantages, and market demand.

To maximize income potential and occupancy rates, setting competitive rental prices necessitates a strategic strategy that includes market intelligence, property evaluation, tenant preferences, and pricing flexibility. Landlords and property managers can effectively navigate the rental market landscape, draw in qualified tenants, and achieve sustainable rental income growth by using tools for comparative market analysis, dynamic pricing strategies, and understanding market dynamics. In addition to increasing the property's value and improving tenant attractiveness, strategic pricing selections help rental properties stand out from the competition, increase tenant satisfaction, and foster long-term success in real estate investments and property management ventures.

CHAPTER VII

Tenant Management

Screening and selecting tenants

The act of screening and choosing renters is the first step in tenant management. This procedure is critical to a happy renting experience, risk reduction, and preservation of property value. Thorough evaluation standards, adherence to the law, and ethical considerations are all part of an efficient tenant screening process that finds eligible candidates who exhibit sound financial management, dependability, and suitability for honoring leases and preserving the integrity of the property.

To evaluate potential tenants consistently and fairly while adhering to fair housing rules and regulations, it is imperative to establish screening criteria that are both objective and unambiguous. To determine an applicant's eligibility and financial stability, landlords and property managers set minimal standards, including income verification, credit history, rental history, work status, and criminal background checks. To ensure openness and adherence to nondiscriminatory methods that protect tenant rights and preserve legal requirements, screening criteria may vary depending on the type of property, rental market conditions, and landlord preferences.

To ascertain a prospective tenant's capacity to pay rent and adhere to lease terms, financial verification and credit history assessment offer valuable insights into their creditworthiness, debt responsibilities, and stability. To assess payment histories, outstanding debts, and credit ratings that reflect financial responsibility and dependability in fulfilling financial obligations, landlords request proof of income, verify employment, and examine credit reports. Landlords can make well-informed decisions to protect their property assets and reduce financial risk by evaluating debt-to-income ratios, past rental payment records, and adverse credit history.

Tenant dependability, adherence to the terms of the lease, and property upkeep throughout prior tenancies can be confirmed by looking over rental history and getting in touch with prior landlords or property management firms. To evaluate potential tenants' rental behavior and eligibility for occupancy, landlords enquire about their prompt rental payments, property maintenance routines, adherence to the lease, and reasons for moving. Obtaining tenant references provides direct insights into tenant conduct, communication skills, and interpersonal interactions that influence tenant-manager relationships and property management efficiency.

To evaluate an applicant's capacity to make regular rent payments throughout the lease, employment verification verifies the applicant's current employment status, income stability, and length of employment. To verify applicants' sources of income, job stability, and ability to pay rent, landlords may ask for employment verification letters, pay stubs, or tax returns. Tenant selection selections that favor reliable revenue sources and minimize rental payment risks are informed by an evaluation of applicants' employment history, career trajectory, and potential for future income growth.

Criminal background checks are compliant with legal standards and guarantee community well-being, property security, and tenant safety. To protect their investment, the peace of the community, or the well-being of their tenants, landlords screen potential renters for criminal convictions, offenses, or histories. Respecting local, state, and federal housing regulations forbids discrimination based on criminal background while balancing tenant screening goals—preserving residential standards, safeguarding property investments, and preserving tenant privacy and rights.

Tenant screening procedures are guided by fair housing standards and ethical concerns, which support nondiscriminatory behavior, equality of opportunity, and the preservation of tenant rights. Fair housing rules, which forbid discrimination based on race, color, religion, national origin, sex, familial status, handicap, or other protected characteristics in tenant selection, leasing decisions, and rental practices, are upheld by landlords and property managers. Standardized application processes, records of applicant communications, and secrecy all help to guarantee adherence to fair housing laws, build rapport with potential renters, and encourage inclusive rental policies that respect moral principles and communal peace.

Establishing shared expectations for lease agreements and property management duties, as well as fostering transparency and clarifying leasing conditions, are all made possible through effective communication with potential renters. To help tenants make well-informed decisions and expedite the tenant selection process, landlords give applicants precise rental requirements, application procedures, and timeline expectations. Clear communication of the lease terms, rental policies, and tenant duties foster mutual respect understanding, and the development of tenant-manager solid relationships based on mutual trust and cooperation.

The first steps in tenant management involve screening and choosing renters based on thorough assessment standards, legal observance, and moral principles that protect real estate investments, reduce hazards, and foster satisfying renting experiences. Landlords and property managers find qualified applicants who exhibit dependability, financial responsibility, and suitability to uphold lease agreements and maintain property integrity by establishing clear screening criteria, carrying out extensive background checks, confirming financial stability, and abiding by fair housing laws. In a variety of dynamic rental markets, efficient tenant screening procedures promote long-term rental success, tenant happiness, and superior property management by cultivating relationships between tenants and managers based on openness, trust, and respect

Creating lease agreements

A key component of property management is drafting lease agreements, which specify legal requirements, clarify rights for tenants, and provide operational instructions for a positive landlord-tenant relationship for the duration of the lease. An effective lease agreement protects the interests of both parties and acts as a legally enforceable contract between landlords and tenants. It outlines the terms of occupation, financial obligations, property regulations, and dispute resolution processes.

Tenant and landlord rights and obligations are made clear by the fundamental elements included in lease agreements. The property address, lease length, rental amount, due dates for payments, security deposit requirements, utilities, maintenance responsibilities, pet restrictions, occupancy limitations, and lease renewal or termination clauses are some of these components. Landlords can avoid potential conflicts, set clear expectations, and guarantee compliance with local housing laws and regulatory requirements governing rental homes by addressing these elements in detail.

Ensuring the lease agreement contains a comprehensive property description permits the tenant to precisely identify the leased premises, including the rooms, facilities, and common areas they can use. Through move-in inspection reports, inventory lists, and photographic documentation, landlords record the condition of their properties. They also note any existing damages, furnishings, and appliances made available by tenants. To maintain the state of the property and adhere to the conditions of the lease, tenants are notified of their responsibilities to maintain cleanliness, take care of fixtures, and report maintenance issues as soon as they arise by describing the property's features and outlining maintenance duties.

The monthly rental amount, the date of payment, the accepted modes of payment, and the policies for late payments and penalties for past-due rent are all outlined in terms of rent payment. To ensure timely payments and prevent cash flow problems, landlords explain expectations for rent submission and specify appropriate payment methods, such as bank transfers, checks, or internet payments. By establishing repercussions for late rent payments that affect property operations and financial stability, late fees or penalty rules encourage rent compliance and prompt payment.

The terms of security deposits delineate the amount amassed, approved applications, terms for reimbursement, and protocols for deducting deposits upon the expiration of the lease. Landlords record deposit amounts, restrictions particular to each state, and disclosure obligations about the processing of deposits, the accrual of interest, and itemized deductions for damages beyond typical wear and tear. Ensuring equitable treatment of security deposits, transparency, and adherence to legal requirements for tenant security are facilitated by keeping security deposits safe in escrow accounts, furnishing renters with deposit receipts, and performing move-in and move-out inspections.

Tenant responsibilities specify duties about the usage of the property, upkeep requirements, noise limits, trash removal, and following community guidelines that protect the property's value and guarantee tenant accountability. To encourage tenant cooperation, maintain the property's aesthetics, and enforce the conditions of the lease agreement, which protect the property's condition and tenant satisfaction for the duration of the tenancy, landlords set rules for lawn care, pest control, and seasonal maintenance duties.

Landlords are shielded from legal ramifications, regulatory penalties, and tenant disputes resulting from noncompliance with fair housing, eviction protocols, habitability standards, and lease termination rules by ensuring that lease agreements adhere to federal, state, and local housing laws. To uphold legal obligations, tenant rights, and procedural fairness in lease enforcement, landlords incorporate statutory disclosures, rights-to-entry provisions, and notices of rent increases. These termination clauses correspond with jurisdiction-specific rental laws, and eviction moratoriums.

To settle disputes amicably and save expensive litigation, dispute resolution clauses specify the processes for resolving problems, grievances, or breach of lease issues through mediation, arbitration, or legal action. Conditions for early lease termination, notice obligations, alternatives for lease buyouts, and repercussions for lease violations or tenant abandonment that involve property vacancy, re-rental efforts, and turnover costs are all outlined in the lease termination terms. Clear instructions, provisions for mutual agreement, and legal protections that facilitate lease termination procedures guarantee smooth property turnover, reduce financial risk, and promote property management operations continuity.

Drafting complete lease agreements entails defining tenant rights, establishing reciprocal obligations, and safeguarding property interests through fair procedures, regulatory compliance, and unambiguous language.

Landlords create operational guidelines that support tenant satisfaction, property maintenance, and regulatory compliance throughout the lease term by addressing crucial elements like rental terms, property descriptions, payment policies, security deposits, tenant responsibilities, legal compliance, dispute resolution, and lease termination. Properly drafted lease agreements facilitate successful tenancy experiences and sustainable property management practices in various rental markets by promoting openness, minimizing conflicts, and supporting good communication between the landlord and tenant.

Handling tenant issues and conflicts

Managing tenant issues and conflicts is a crucial component of property management to preserve good landlord-tenant relations and guarantee property compliance. This involves proactive communication, conflict resolution techniques, and adherence to legal requirements. Landlords and property managers employ strategies that prioritize tenant satisfaction, uphold lease agreements, and mitigate potential risks to property integrity and community harmony to navigate various challenges, including maintenance requests, lease violations, neighbor disputes, and communication breakdowns.

Ensuring tenant happiness and maintaining property upkeep requires prompt attention to maintenance requests. To preserve property conditions and prevent maintenance issues from worsening, landlords set clear protocols for tenants to report maintenance difficulties. They also prioritize urgent repairs that threaten the safety or habitability of the property and plan routine maintenance chores. In addition to demonstrating a dedication to tenant welfare and upholding property management standards that increase tenant retention and property value, efficient communication channels, service request tracking systems, and attentive maintenance personnel guarantee the prompt resolution of maintenance concerns.

To settle disagreements over shared amenities, parking disputes, noise disruptions, property boundaries, or other issues that affect tenant comfort and community harmony, neighbors must be mediated with tact, objectivity, and effective communication. To promote mutual respect, reduce tension, and foster a cooperative living environment that supports tenant well-being and neighborhood cohesion, landlords should provide opportunities for open dialogue between disputing parties, clarify expectations regarding noise regulations, parking policies, and shared space etiquette, and implement preventive measures like community rules enforcement and conflict resolution workshops.

Maintaining consistency, fairness, and adherence to the lease agreement terms are necessary when enforcing property policies and lease violations. These include tenant noncompliance with rental obligations, unauthorized subletting, pet policy violations, and property misuse that endangers safety or disturbs community peace. When necessary, by the terms of the lease and applicable laws, landlords serve official notifications, record lease violations, and explain the consequences of noncompliance through warnings, lease revisions, or eviction procedures. Encouraging tenant accountability, bolstering lease enforcement, and preserving the integrity of property management are all facilitated by clear communication of expectations, consequences, and corrective actions.

To resolve misconceptions, miscommunications, or language hurdles obstructing productive landlord-tenant interactions, proactive involvement, active listening, and conflict resolution skills are necessary when navigating communication breakdowns. Tenant issues, lease clarification, and fast dispute resolution are all handled by landlords through many channels of communication, open lines of communication, and scheduled check-ins. This way, problems are resolved before they worsen, affecting tenant happiness or lease compliance. Long-term tenant retention and successful property management are supported by fostering strong tenant relations, establishing trust, and exhibiting empathy when resolving tenant complaints. These actions also facilitate dispute resolution, enhance mutual understanding, and encourage collaborative problem-solving.

To accommodate renters facing temporary financial issues or unforeseen circumstances that affect their capacity to pay rent, managing rent arrears and financial hardships requires empathetic communication, financial assistance programs, and rent repayment arrangements. To create reasonable payback agreements that prioritize rent duties, prevent eviction, and support tenant retention while guaranteeing financial stability for property operations, landlords interact with tenants, discuss rental assistance resources, and offer flexible payment options. Tenant-landlord relationships are maintained during uncertain economic times by enforcing lease compliance, reducing the risk of rent arrears, using proactive rent-collecting tactics, monitoring payment compliance, and offering tenant support services.

Legal remedies or mediation require objective assessment, adherence to lease conditions, and compliance with statutory dispute resolution procedures to resolve irreconcilable conflicts, lease disputes, or claims of breach of contract. Regarding safeguarding property interests, preserving tenant rights, and adhering to rental laws, landlords can arrange mediation sessions, assign third parties to mediate disputes or confer with legal counsel to negotiate settlements, explain legal rights, and enforce lease agreements through court processes.

In addition to preserving landlord-tenant relationships and reducing the danger of litigation, swift, professional, and equitable conflict resolution fosters a positive rental environment that places a premium on respect for one another, tenant satisfaction, and effective property management.

To handle maintenance requests, mediate neighbor disputes, enforce lease violations, navigate communication breakdowns, manage rent arrears, and resolve disputes through mediation or legal recourse effectively, managing tenant issues and conflicts requires proactive communication, conflict resolution skills, and adherence to legal guidelines. Landlords and property managers create a favorable living environment, cultivate positive landlord-tenant relationships, and ensure sustainable property management practices that support long-term tenant retention and property value in a variety of rental markets by putting into practice strategies that prioritize tenant satisfaction, uphold lease agreements and mitigate potential risks to property integrity and community harmony.

Ensuring tenant retention and satisfaction

Maintaining a steady rental income stream, reducing vacancies, and cultivating a favorable reputation in the cutthroat rental market depends heavily on tenant retention and satisfaction. To encourage long-term tenancy and the property's sustainability, landlords and property managers take proactive measures to improve the tenant experience, foster solid landlord-tenant relationships, and immediately attend to tenant demands.

Greeting new renters and ensuring their move-in goes well are the first steps in creating an excellent first impression. To provide a smooth transition and encourage tenant comfort, landlords offer thorough move-in orientations, highlight property features, amenities, and neighborhood resources, and respond to tenant questions. Establishing expectations, fostering trust, and reaffirming a commitment to tenant happiness and superior property management are all made possible by clear communication of lease terms, property policies, and maintenance schedules.

To show a dedication to tenant welfare and property care, it is imperative to respond to tenant inquiries, maintenance requests, and complaints swiftly through responsive communication and accessibility. To support effective issue resolution and foster tenant confidence in property management responsiveness, landlords should set up clear lines of communication, swiftly respond to communications from tenants, and offer several contact options, such as phone, email, or online portals. Proactive involvement, frequent check-ins, and transparent updates on property concerns support effective tenant-landlord interactions. These actions also strengthen tenant satisfaction, build confidence, and promote open communication.

To handle maintenance issues quickly and stop property deterioration, proactive property maintenance and upkeep schedules regular inspections, preventive maintenance chores, and timely repairs. This preserves the property's beauty, functionality, and tenant comfort. Seasonal property inspections, early maintenance requests, and investments in repairs and enhancements that increase tenant quality of life, energy efficiency, and overall property appeal are all carried out by landlords. In competitive rental markets, keeping common areas, landscaping, and amenities clean and well-maintained encourages pride of residency, encourages tenant retention, and supports property value appreciation.

Improving community involvement and amenity quality creates a desirable living space that draws and keeps renters looking for top-notch amenities, recreational opportunities, and socializing spots. To accommodate tenant preferences and encourage active lifestyles, landlords invest in amenities like fitness centers, swimming pools, common areas, and pet-friendly housing. Tenant engagement, linkages to the community, and a sense of belonging are all strengthened by planning social events, neighborhood projects, and community gatherings. These factors increase tenant satisfaction and support long-term tenancy.

By considering changing tenant demands and preferences, providing variable lease terms and renewal incentives encourages tenants to renew their leases, rewards long-term residence, and fosters tenant loyalty. To promote timely lease renewals and reduce turnover costs, landlords give options for lease renewal, go over lease conditions in advance, and provide incentives like rental discounts, upgrading options, or lease extension bonuses. Tenant retention is bolstered by landlord-tenant relationships based on mutual respect and trust, strengthened by flexibility in lease terms, prompt lease management, and lease negotiation that shows a commitment to tenant retention.

Inquiring about tenant comments and implementing continuous improvement plans show that a property is attentive to its guests' needs, wants, and recommendations for improving its features, services, and overall operational effectiveness. To find areas for improvement, close service gaps, and put into practice workable solutions that will enhance tenant experience and operational excellence, landlords prioritize tenant input in decision-making processes, conduct tenant satisfaction surveys, and request feedback on property management practices. Tenant empowerment, resident contentment, and a cooperative tenant-manager relationship are all enhanced when tenant feedback is included in property management practices. These factors support both long-term tenant retention and the performance of the property.

To handle tenant complaints, lease disputes, or other issues professionally and respectfully, dispute resolution and conflict management prioritize fairness, communication, and mediation. To settle disputes, uphold the conditions of the lease, and maintain the tenant-landlord relationship, landlords encourage candid communication, pay close attention to tenant concerns, and work together to find mutually acceptable solutions. In addition to upholding tenant rights, maintaining procedural fairness, and maintaining the integrity of property management, offering alternative dispute resolution options and avoiding turnover risks associated with unresolved disputes also entails hiring third-party mediators and abiding by legal requirements.

To maintain long-term property success and foster strong landlord-tenant relationships, proactive management methods, timely communication, and a dedication to tenant welfare, property care, and community involvement are necessary for tenant retention and satisfaction. Landlords and property managers can cultivate a favorable living environment, attract and retain quality tenants in competitive rental markets, and establish a reputation for excellence in property management by establishing positive first impressions, upholding property integrity, improving amenities, providing flexible lease terms, asking for tenant feedback, and resolving disputes respectfully.

CHAPTER VIII

Maintenance and Property Management

Regular maintenance tasks and schedules

To maintain the integrity of the property, improve tenant happiness, and reduce operational disturbances, thorough schedules for everyday chores must be established for effective maintenance and property management. To minimize hazards, preserve property value, and provide renters with a secure and functional living environment, landlords and property managers prioritize property upkeep, implement proactive maintenance measures, and comply with legal requirements.

Routine inspection and assessment serve as fundamental elements of property management by determining maintenance needs, assessing property conditions, and resolving problems before they worsen. To look for wear, damage, or degradation indications, landlords regularly inspect the roofing, structural elements, HVAC systems, plumbing fixtures, electrical components, and outside and interior regions. In addition to facilitating proactive maintenance planning and ensuring compliance with regulatory requirements and property maintenance standards, the documentation of inspection findings, maintenance logs, and photographic recordings also helps to prioritize repair needs.

HVAC systems maintenance includes routine inspections, filter replacements, cleaning, and preventive maintenance to maximize system efficiency, enhance indoor air quality, and prolong equipment lifespan. To reduce energy consumption, avoid expensive repairs, and guarantee tenant comfort during fluctuating weather conditions, landlords arrange periodic HVAC inspections, carry out routine filter changes, and immediately handle system failures. Property managers may encourage sustainable practices that save operating costs and improve tenant satisfaction by implementing HVAC system maintenance contracts, monitoring system performance metrics, and switching to more energy-efficient equipment.

Landlords schedule periodic plumbing inspections, promptly address leaks, and upgrade plumbing fixtures to improve water efficiency and mitigate water-related risks. Maintaining plumbing and electrical systems involves checking pipes, fixtures, faucets, and electrical components for leaks, corrosion, or malfunction. Electrical system maintenance includes replacing lighting fixtures with energy-efficient models, checking outlets, circuit breakers, and wiring for safety compliance, and handling electrical problems to improve operational dependability and property safety.

As part of property preservation activities, routine roof inspections, gutter cleaning, siding repairs, and exterior painting safeguard homes from weather factors, moisture penetration, and structural damage. Landlords are responsible for maintaining curb appeal, structural integrity, and weather-resistant property exteriors that survive environmental challenges. They also preserve curb appeal by doing periodic gutter maintenance to avoid debris buildup and inspecting roof shingles, flashing, and drainage systems.

To encourage outdoor enjoyment and community aesthetics, groundskeeping and landscape care schedule lawn mowing, irrigation system maintenance, tree pruning, and seasonal landscaping additions. These actions improve property aesthetics, curb appeal, and tenant satisfaction. To save water, save maintenance expenses, and create hospitable outdoor places that enhance tenant life and draw in potential tenants, landlords prioritize landscape maintenance duties, employ sustainable landscaping techniques, and use drought-tolerant plants.

Upgrading and maintaining kitchen appliances, laundry facilities, and other equipment is necessary to maintain optimal performance, reduce energy usage, and increase the longevity of appliances. To enhance tenant convenience, save utility costs, and adhere to energy efficiency regulations promoting sustainable property management practices, landlords plan appliance inspections, perform preventative maintenance, and replace antiquated appliances with energy-efficient versions.

Emergency readiness and response processes protect tenant safety, property assets, and operational continuity by putting emergency preparedness plans into action, practicing drills, and keeping necessary supplies on hand to reduce the risk of natural catastrophes, fires, or security events. To increase tenant safety awareness, expedite prompt emergency response, and minimize property damage during unanticipated situations, landlords install smoke detectors, carbon monoxide alarms, and fire extinguishers, give emergency contact information, and instruct renters on evacuation protocols.

Adhering to building codes, zoning laws, health and safety laws, and environmental regulations that control property upkeep, tenant occupancy, and operational procedures is part of complying with regulatory standards. To ensure their property complies with local, state, and federal rules, landlords maintain up-to-date knowledge of regulatory revisions, secure the required permits for upgrades, and do inspections. To reduce liability risks, preserve property management integrity by industry best practices and regulatory guidelines, and demonstrate devotion to legal obligations, keeping correct records, using licensed contractors, and swiftly handling compliance issues are important.

Proactive planning, routine maintenance, and regulation compliance are all parts of maintenance and property management. These practices protect the integrity of the property, improve tenant satisfaction, and foster long-term property value growth. Landlords and property managers can ensure operational efficiency, mitigate risks, and promote a safe and functional living environment that supports tenant retention and property sustainability in competitive rental markets by putting comprehensive maintenance schedules into place, conducting routine inspections, promptly attending to maintenance needs, and placing a high priority on tenant safety.

Handling emergency repairs

An essential part of property management is responding quickly to unforeseen events jeopardizing tenant safety, property integrity, and business continuity. This calls for readiness, efficient communication, and quick action. To reduce hazards, protect tenant welfare, and preserve property management standards in an emergency, landlords and property managers put emergency response plans into place, prioritize necessary repairs, and keep essential supplies on hand.

For proactive preparedness and quick action in the case of an emergency—such as a fire, flood, severe weather event, or structural damage endangering the safety of tenants or property assets—it is imperative to establish emergency response protocols. To enable quick response, reduce property damage, and guarantee tenant safety in emergencies, landlords create thorough emergency plans, provide tenants with emergency contact information, and specify protocols for reporting emergencies, leaving the property, and contacting emergency services.

Tenant safety and communication should be prioritized. This entails quickly evaluating emergency circumstances, informing impacted tenants, and giving clear directions on evacuation routes, emergency exits, and safety precautions to reduce risks and enable a smooth evacuation if needed. To encourage tenant knowledge, composure, and cooperation in stressful times, landlords keep lines of communication open, set up emergency communication systems, and inform tenants of service outages, evacuation orders, and emergency response measures.

When it comes to plumbing leaks, electrical outages, HVAC problems, or structural damage that jeopardizes the property's performance, tenant comfort, and operational continuity, critical maintenance concerns must be addressed immediately. To stabilize the situation, stop additional property damage, and restore vital services that enable tenant occupancy and property operations, landlords prioritize emergency maintenance requests, send out competent contractors or maintenance staff, and carry out temporary repairs.

When handling emergencies requiring expert assistance or specific equipment, coordination with emergency service providers—such as fire departments, utility companies, and restoration specialists—ensures prompt involvement, specialized knowledge, and regulatory compliance. To accelerate property restoration efforts, minimize liabilities, and guarantee adherence to safety standards during emergency repairs, landlords build agreements with reputable service providers, keep contact information for emergency responders, and work together on emergency response plans.

To support insurance claims processing, regulatory compliance, and the post-event assessment of response efficacy, emergency response procedures documentation entails keeping thorough records of emergencies, response activities taken, communication exchanges, and repair documentation. To improve emergency readiness, expedite response efforts, and increase property management practices that prioritize tenant safety and operational resilience, landlords update emergency response plans in response to lessons learned, tenant feedback, or regulatory changes.

To avoid theft, vandalism, and illegal entrance during repair and restoration activities, temporary security measures must be implemented, access to impacted areas must be restricted, and intact property assets must be protected. To safeguard tenant property, preserve the integrity of the building, and provide a secure working environment for emergency responders and contractors, landlords manage property access, keep an eye out for security flaws, and deploy security guards or surveillance systems as needed.

To mitigate long-term effects and restore the property, comprehensive repair plans must be developed, post-emergency assessments must be completed, structural damages must be assessed, and tenant occupancy and property operations must be minimized. To minimize financial losses, speed property recovery, and rebuild tenant confidence in property management response, landlords prioritize permanent repairs, arrange follow-up inspections, and communicate restoration timelines to tenants, insurers, and regulatory agencies.

To optimize disaster response speed and effectiveness, ongoing training, scenario simulations, proactive measures, and updated emergency supplies and communication techniques must continuously improve emergency readiness. To increase property management resilience, reduce emergency risks, and foster a safe and secure living environment that supports tenant retention and property value in various rental markets, landlords should ask tenants for feedback, evaluate emergency response performance, and incorporate lessons learned into emergency preparedness plans.

Proactive preparation, quick thinking, and clear communication are necessary for handling emergency repairs to preserve property assets, ensure tenant safety, and keep operations running smoothly in unforeseen circumstances. A landlord or property manager can guarantee tenant satisfaction and long-term property viability in dynamic rental environments by implementing emergency response protocols, prioritizing tenant welfare, coordinating with emergency service providers, documenting response procedures, securing property assets, and facilitating property restoration. These actions show a commitment to tenant protection, regulatory compliance, and excellence in property management.

Hiring and working with property managers

Hiring and collaborating with property managers is a wise strategic move for landlords looking to maximize returns on their real estate investments, streamline processes, and guarantee efficient day-to-day management of rental properties. In addition to providing knowledge, industry insights, and operational efficiency that promote long-term property success, property managers are invaluable collaborators who look after property owners' interests in maintenance, tenant relations, financial management, and regulatory compliance.

The first step in determining whether you require professional management is to evaluate the property's size, the rental portfolio's complexity, your availability to manage day-to-day operations efficiently, tenant relations, and maintenance needs. To reduce management responsibilities, increase property profitability, and take advantage of professional management expertise in navigating rental market dynamics, landlords consider several factors, including time constraints, property management skills, and a desire for hands-on involvement in property operations, before hiring a property manager.

Property managers possess a wide range of skills and knowledge necessary for efficient property management and tenant satisfaction, including familiarity with local rental market trends, regulatory requirements, property maintenance procedures, tenant screening protocols, and financial management concepts. Property managers with a track record of successfully managing rental properties, relevant experience, industry certifications, and a dedication to providing outstanding customer service, cultivating tenant-landlord relationships, and optimizing property investment potential through proactive management techniques and operational excellence are highly sought after by landlords.

When choosing a property manager, it's essential to carry out in-depth interviews, verify references, and evaluate the candidate's managerial abilities, communication skills, and compatibility with the objectives and goals of property management. To find the best fit for property management needs, operational requirements, and long-term investment objectives, prioritizing property performance and owner peace of mind, landlords assess property management fees, service offerings, tenant retention rates, and responsiveness to emergencies.

To maintain transparency, accountability, and alignment with property owner objectives, it is imperative to establish clear expectations and responsibilities that clearly define the scope of property management activities, performance metrics, communication procedures, and reporting requirements. To formally set expectations, clarify responsibilities, and protect property interests by legal requirements and industry standards, landlords draft comprehensive property management agreements that include information on leasing procedures, maintenance standards, financial reporting timelines, eviction protocols, and dispute resolution procedures.

Building positive working relationships, resolving property issues, and making well-informed decisions that affect the profitability of properties and tenant satisfaction all depend on landlords and property managers working together and communicating well. Regular communication channels—such as email updates, scheduled meetings, and property management software platforms—allow for real-time updates on property operations, financial performance, tenant issues, and maintenance activities to maximize property management efficiency and tenant retention. These updates are contingent upon landlord input, approval, or strategic guidance.

Budgeting, rent collection, spending tracking, lease renewals, property tax payments, and financial statements that give landlords insight into property income, expenses, and profitability metrics are all included in financial management and reporting. Property managers uphold precise financial documentation, conform to budgetary directives, balance accounts payable and receivable, and compile exhaustive financial summaries that empower landlords to make informed decisions based on data, evaluate the performance of their properties, and maximize income streams using proactive financial management strategies in line with investment objectives.

Guarantee property compliance, tenant safety, operational efficiency, maintenance monitoring, and vendor management entails organizing regular maintenance chores, emergency repairs, and property inspections. Property maintenance of property aesthetics, functionality, and regulatory compliance standards that promote tenant satisfaction and property value appreciation is the responsibility of property managers, who also arrange maintenance services, get competitive bids from licensed contractors, and supervise vendor performance, quality assurance, and adherence to service agreements.

To promote good tenant-landlord relations, reduce tenant turnover, and guarantee lease compliance, tenant relations and lease administration include tenant screening, lease negotiations, rent collection, lease enforcement, and resolving tenant questions or complaints. To maintain property profitability and the success of long-term investments, property managers perform comprehensive tenant screenings, manage communications with tenants, enforce lease terms, and employ tenant retention strategies that increase tenant satisfaction, lower vacancy rates, and maximize occupancy levels.

To reduce liability risks, safeguard property interests, and guarantee adherence to legal standards that regulate property management operations, legal compliance and risk management necessitate navigating landlord-tenant legislation, fair housing regulations, eviction procedures, and property insurance requirements. To protect property assets, tenant welfare, and landlord reputation in competitive rental markets, property managers stay current on regulatory changes, secure the required permits, licenses, and insurance, and put risk mitigation strategies, emergency preparedness plans, and property security measures into practice.

Employing and collaborating with property managers gives landlords a competitive edge in maximizing investment potential, streamlining operations, and guaranteeing tenant satisfaction through professional property management, proactive approaches to management, and observance of legal and regulatory requirements that promote long-term property success in ever-changing rental markets. Landlords can leverage professional expertise, streamline property operations, and achieve investment objectives by prioritizing property performance, tenant welfare, and owner peace of mind by choosing qualified property managers, setting clear expectations, encouraging effective communication, and working together on property management goals.

Cost-effective property management strategies

For landlords and property managers who want to keep their properties valued and their tenants happy while improving operational efficiency, cutting costs, and optimizing returns on investment, cost-effective property management techniques are essential. Property stakeholders can attain sustained property performance and financial viability in competitive rental markets through proactive management techniques, leveraging technology, prioritizing preventative maintenance, and cultivating tenant connections.

Preventive measures and proactive maintenance are essential for reducing repair costs and increasing the life of a property. Tenant satisfaction is increased, and property integrity is preserved through routine inspections, prompt repairs, and preventative maintenance activities that address problems before they become more serious. Setting priorities for maintenance tasks like roof cleaning, plumbing inspections, and HVAC service minimizes the need for emergency repairs and maximizes the use of available resources, encouraging effective property management techniques that eventually lower operating costs.

Energy efficiency programs save utility costs and increase property value, significantly contributing to cost-effective management. Installing smart thermostats, energy-efficient appliances, and upgraded insulation draws environmentally concerned renters and supports sustainability objectives, cutting overall operating expenses and encouraging environmental stewardship. Landlords may attract tenants who value energy-efficient living spaces by showcasing their commitment to sustainability through green certifications and energy audits.

Automation and technological integration improve workflow efficiency and tenant communication while streamlining property management processes. Rent collection, maintenance requests, and lease administration are made more accessible by property management software, online portals, and automated systems, improving data accuracy and lessening administrative workloads. Landlords may enhance property management performance and support long-term financial goals by optimizing efficiency, scalability, and tenant satisfaction through digital platforms for tenant screening, financial reporting, and marketing.

Setting attainable objectives, keeping an eye on spending, and allocating funds for capital projects and property upgrades are all part of strategic financial planning.

Landlords may secure consistent returns on their property investments even in the face of market swings by using comprehensive budgeting and economic forecasts to discover cost-saving possibilities, prioritize investments, and maximize cash flow. Landlords can reduce financial risks and eventually increase the profitability of their properties by adhering to a strict budget and changing their tactics in response to shifting market conditions.

Retaining tenants is essential to lowering turnover expenses and vacancy rates, increasing rental income, and operational effectiveness. Long-term tenant relationships are fostered, and tenant satisfaction is improved through efficient tenant involvement, prompt communication, and specialized services. Incentives for lease renewals, property improvements based on tenant input, and quick problem-solving help create a happy tenant experience, reduce turnover-related costs, and steady occupancy levels.

Risk management techniques to minimize liability risks and safeguard property assets include comprehending regulatory requirements, securing sufficient insurance coverage, and implementing safety procedures. Landlords prioritize tenant screenings, maintain property security, and comply with landlord-tenant rules to reduce legal issues and potential financial losses. Landlords protect their economic interests in a competitive rental market by maintaining property integrity, ensuring tenant safety, and remaining updated about industry regulations and proactive risk mitigation techniques.

Initiatives for community involvement and focused marketing improve the property's exposure, draw in potential tenants, and fortify the brand's reputation. Property features are highlighted by working with nearby companies, organizing neighborhood gatherings, and using digital marketing tools, and potential long-term renters are drawn in. In competitive marketplaces, effective marketing techniques enhance occupancy rates and property profitability by emphasizing resident testimonials, highlighting property characteristics, and differentiating offerings.

Proactive maintenance, energy efficiency programs, technology integration, strategic financial planning, tenant retention campaigns, risk management techniques, and community involvement programs are all examples of cost-effective property management tactics. Landlords and property managers decrease costs, optimize returns on investment, and optimize property performance by using sustainable management techniques, cultivating tenant contentment, and maintaining regulatory compliance. Property stakeholders may provide value-driven rental experiences, foster operational excellence, and secure long-term financial success in dynamic rental markets by prioritizing efficiency and tenant satisfaction

CHAPTER IX

Legal Considerations and Compliance

Understanding landlord-tenant laws

To preserve legal compliance, safeguard property interests, and promote good tenant relations while reducing legal risks and liabilities, landlords and property managers must be knowledgeable about landlord-tenant regulations. Landlords can promote a fair and transparent rental environment that supports long-term property viability and tenant satisfaction by being aware of these laws' nuances and ensuring they follow the regulations governing rental agreements, property maintenance standards, eviction procedures, and tenant rights.

Detailed lease agreements are essential to define tenant responsibilities, preserve landlord interests, and set clear expectations. Terms about rent payments, length of lease, limitations on how the property may be used, maintenance obligations, and dispute resolution processes are usually included in lease agreements. To reduce uncertainty and legal risks during the tenancy, landlords should create leases that adhere to local laws, clearly identify tenant rights and landlord obligations, and include provisions for rent increases, security deposits, and lease termination conditions.

Fair housing rules, which forbid discrimination based on race, color, religion, national origin, sex, familial status, or handicap, must be followed by tenant screening procedures. Landlords maintain just and equitable tenant selection procedures by reviewing rental histories, credit reports, and background checks for each application. Landlords can protect their reputations, reduce the possibility of discrimination, and comply with local, state, and federal fair housing laws that control tenant selection and screening procedures by following fair housing principles.

The landlord is responsible for keeping rental homes livable and complying with building, health, and safety regulations. Property maintenance includes timely repair, sufficient plumbing, heating, and electrical systems, and provision of necessities like clean water and appropriate waste disposal facilities. If landlords disregard the habitability requirements specified in landlord-tenant regulations, tenants can demand repairs, withhold rent for unsolved maintenance issues, or take legal action.

Rent collection procedures must comply with lease agreements and municipal rent control legislation to prevent disagreements over unpaid rent, late fines, and eviction procedures. In lease agreements, landlords specify the dates, modes of payment, and late penalties for rent, and they make plain to renters what is expected of them in terms of payment. Landlords can uphold financial agreements, foster positive tenant relations, and navigate legal channels effectively to enforce lease terms and protect property income streams by being aware of the procedures regarding rent increases, eviction notices, and tenant rights regarding rent payment disputes.

Landlords must adhere to legal regulations when navigating the eviction process, deliver eviction notifications by state law, and file court cases for lease violations, unpaid rent, or tenant misbehavior. To establish legal claims and fight against tenant challenges in court, landlords must grant tenants the right to due process, follow eviction schedules, and keep meticulous records of all communications and acts relating to eviction proceedings. Landlords can legally settle tenancy conflicts, regain ownership of rental properties, and lessen the financial losses connected with eviction procedures by being aware of eviction rules and legal remedies.

Other than going to court, landlord-tenant disputes can be settled through alternative dispute resolution procedures like mediation or arbitration. Landlords can efficiently handle lease violations, property damages, or arguments over lease conditions by negotiating, hiring legal counsel, or using dispute resolution services. Landlords can protect tenant relations, encourage peaceful outcomes, and reduce legal expenses related to formal court procedures or eviction actions—all of which can affect the effectiveness of property management and tenant satisfaction—by looking into collaborative dispute resolution methods.

For landlords and property managers to successfully handle legal intricacies, preserve tenant rights, and safeguard property interests, they must have a solid understanding of landlord-tenant laws. Landlords can ensure compliance with regulatory requirements, mitigate legal risks, and foster a fair and transparent rental environment that supports positive tenant-landlord relationships and sustainable property management practices in diverse rental markets by studying lease agreements, tenant screening practices, property maintenance standards, rent collection procedures, eviction laws, and dispute resolution mechanisms.

Navigating local and federal regulations

A crucial component of property management and real estate investing is adhering to local and federal regulations, which control many facets of property ownership, rental operations, and tenant relations. Local and federal rules set the legal framework that governs the operations of landlords and property managers. These regulations cover many concerns, from environmental regulations to tenant rights and property upkeep standards. Comprehending these regulations is crucial for steering clear of legal hazards, safeguarding investments in real estate, and cultivating favorable associations with regulatory bodies and tenants.

Local regulations are collectively called ordinances and laws enacted by city or municipal governments that specify zoning restrictions, building codes, rental property registration requirements, and license requirements. These laws can greatly influence management techniques and decisions about real estate investments because they range significantly throughout countries. Landlords must adhere to building rules to maintain property safety and habitability standards and become familiar with local zoning laws to guarantee that properties are used suitably for residential or commercial purposes. Landlords are also required by licensing and registration regulations for rental properties to register their properties with local authorities, receive required licenses, and follow rental housing standards that support the well-being of tenants and the sustainability of their buildings.

Numerous facets of landlord-tenant interactions, fair housing policies, environmental regulations, and financial transactions that affect property management operations are governed by federal legislation. In housing-related activities, such as tenant screening, lease negotiations, and property advertising, discrimination based on race, color, religion, national origin, sex, familial status, or disability is prohibited by the Fair Housing Act. To guarantee equitable housing options for all applicants and prevent legal ramifications for discriminatory acts, landlords must adhere to fair housing rules.

Landlords must abide by environmental protection standards, hazardous waste disposal procedures, and energy efficiency requirements that support sustainable property management practices to comply with ecological rules enforced at the municipal and federal levels. To limit ecological effects, save utility costs, and increase property value, compliance with environmental standards includes resolving lead-based paint dangers, asbestos removal, mold treatment, and implementing energy-efficient renovations. To adhere to legal requirements and promote eco-friendly property management activities, landlords may also need to get environmental permits, carry out environmental assessments, and put pollution control measures into place.

Municipal and federal legislation protects tenant interests, privacy rights, and procedural due process in rental housing transactions. According to landlord-tenant regulations, landlords must give tenants livable conditions, prompt maintenance, privacy safeguards, and advance notice of rent hikes or lease terminations. To comply with federal accessibility standards and promote inclusive housing opportunities, landlords are required by federal laws, such as the Americans with Disabilities Act (ADA), to accommodate tenants with disabilities. This involves making reasonable accommodations and ensuring that properties are accessible to individuals with mobility impairments.

Landlords have financial and tax compliance responsibilities that include reporting rental revenue, keeping correct financial records, and abiding by tax laws about real estate investments and rental income reporting. To maximize tax advantages and reduce financial obligations related to property ownership, landlords must submit yearly tax returns, claim deductions for qualified property-related costs, and adhere to IRS regulations regarding depreciation, capital gains, and rental property deductions. Landlords are better equipped to plan for property expenses, maximize returns on investment, and manage cash flow in compliance with federal tax regulations when aware of the tax implications and financial reporting obligations.

Landlords must remain aware of how local and federal laws, regulations, and policy developments affect property management operations to navigate regulatory updates and changes. For information on regulatory changes impacting rental housing, landlord responsibilities, tenant protections, and compliance requirements, landlords can consult the websites of local governments, housing agencies, industry associations, and legal counsel. To reduce risks and protect real estate assets in ever-changing regulatory environments, landlords should adapt management methods, make the required adjustments, and uphold legal compliance by actively monitoring regulatory updates and consulting with experts.

Landlords and property managers must navigate local and federal rules to maintain tenant rights, safeguard property investments, and maintain legal compliance in rental housing operations. Landlords can effectively manage properties, reduce legal risks, and cultivate positive tenant-landlord relationships that support sustainable property management practices and long-term investment success in a variety of rental markets by being aware of local zoning laws, federal fair housing regulations, environmental standards, tenant rights protections, and financial and tax compliance requirements.

Eviction processes and tenant rights

Landlords and property managers must understand eviction procedures and tenant rights to properly navigate legal procedures, fulfill their landlord obligations, and guarantee equitable treatment of tenants throughout the rental agreement. To preserve tenant rights and stop illegal eviction practices, evictions are significant legal acts that must follow specific legal standards, such as notice periods, grounds for eviction, and procedural due process. Landlords can reduce risks, settle conflicts, and uphold compliance with legal requirements that regulate landlord-tenant interactions by being knowledgeable about eviction laws.

Tenant misbehavior that violates rental agreements or lease terms, nonpayment of rent, lease expiration, or lease violations are the usual causes of eviction procedures. By state and local eviction regulations, landlords must provide specific justifications for eviction, such as nonpayment of rent, damage to property, unlawful activity on the property, or breach of lease conditions. Landlords must follow legislative standards that specify eviction dates and procedural steps to ensure proper eviction procedures. They must also keep track of lease violations, give written notices to tenants stating grounds for eviction, and document infractions before starting eviction proceedings.

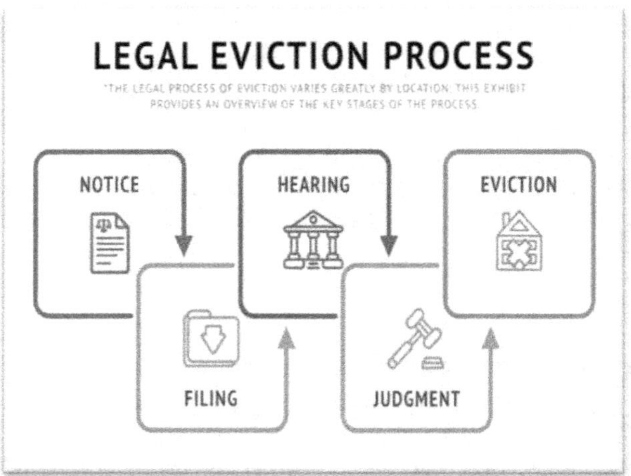

Tenants who receive eviction notices are formally notified of lease violations or other noncompliance issues that may result in eviction procedures. Depending on the jurisdiction and the eviction grounds (such as nonpayment of rent, lease violations, or terminations), different notice requirements and dates apply. To begin formal eviction proceedings, landlords are required by state law to furnish tenants with written notifications that identify the grounds for eviction, stipulate notice periods for corrective action or lease termination, and follow all other notice requirements. Landlords protect tenant rights, give due process, and carry out eviction procedures in compliance with the law when they follow notice requirements.

Tenants are guaranteed the right to fight eviction claims in court, respond to eviction notices, and defend against eviction measures through procedural due process. To achieve an eviction decision, landlords must file eviction lawsuits in court, serve eviction summonses and complaints to tenants, and provide proof to support their claims. Before eviction judgments are executed, tenants can contest accusations, raise defenses, negotiate settlement agreements, ask for more time to correct lease violations, or take care of outstanding debts.

Landlord misconduct, habitability issues, retaliatory eviction allegations, contract compliance, and procedural errors that infringe tenant rights are just a few of the legal defenses tenants may raise against eviction proceedings. Common defenses include discrimination against renters based on protected characteristics under fair housing legislation, inaccurate eviction notices, illegal retribution against tenants, and landlords who fail to maintain habitable conditions. To fight against eviction actions and safeguard their rights throughout legal proceedings, tenants may contest eviction claims in court, request hearings, provide evidence supporting their defenses, and hire an attorney.

Tenants and landlords can settle eviction cases amicably outside of formal court procedures by using alternative dispute resolution techniques like mediation or arbitration. Through the negotiation of settlement conditions, discussion of issues, and mutually accepted settlements to eviction problems, mediation helps parties avoid expensive litigation, maintains tenant-landlord relationships, and fosters effective conflict resolution. Tenants and landlords can work together to find compromise solutions, clear up any misunderstandings, and reach fair agreements that serve the interests of both parties during mediation sessions led by qualified mediators.

Landlords and property managers must comprehend tenant rights and eviction procedures to handle legal difficulties, fulfill legal requirements, and sustain moral standards in the rental housing industry. Landlords can effectively manage eviction proceedings, reduce legal risks, and promote fair and lawful eviction practices that uphold tenant protections and support landlord responsibilities in various rental markets by following eviction laws, giving proper notice, respecting tenant rights, and considering alternative dispute resolution options.

Protecting yourself legally

As a landlord or property manager, you must be aware of potential legal hazards, follow all applicable regulations, and take proactive steps to protect your interests, reduce your liability, and treat renters fairly if you want to be legally protected. Landlords can mitigate legal issues, maintain ethical standards, and encourage lawful property management practices that support long-term rental property success by negotiating legal complications, keeping documents up to date, and cultivating excellent tenant relations.

In addition to overseeing financial transactions, lease agreements, property upkeep, tenant rights protection, and compliance with local, state, and federal laws governing rental housing operations, landlords and property managers also bear legal duties. Knowing the laws governing landlord-tenant relationships, fair housing policies, eviction processes, property maintenance requirements, and environmental regulations that affect property management choices and responsibilities is essential to recognizing legal hazards. Landlords can proactively handle legal difficulties, limit risks, and safeguard property investments against potential liabilities or legal disputes by remaining aware of industry standards and regulatory requirements.

To define tenant rights, outline landlord obligations, describe lease terms, and create legal safeguards for both parties, thorough lease agreements must be drafted. Rent payment terms, security deposit requirements, limitations on how the property may be used, maintenance obligations, eviction procedures, and dispute resolution methods that uphold state laws and safeguard landlord interests should all be included in lease agreements. Landlords can limit legal issues and ensure tenant satisfaction during the tenancy by enforcing lease terms that are clear and enforceable, resolving conflicts, and preventing misconceptions. They can also enforce lease terms in compliance with legal rules.

Maintaining accurate records, monitoring lease agreements, recording tenant interactions, and preserving evidence for future legal issues or litigation all depend on the documentation of communications, financial transactions, and property-related activities. To substantiate legal claims, prove adherence to lease provisions, and mount a strong defense against tenant challenges or legal actions, landlords should retain copies of lease agreements, rental applications, correspondence with tenants, repair requests, maintenance records, rent payment receipts, and eviction notices. Landlords may maintain openness in property management operations, handle rental properties efficiently, and immediately answer tenant inquiries when they follow organized documentation standards.

Landlords with insurance coverage are shielded from lawsuits, property damage, liability claims, and unanticipated expenses brought on by damaged property, crises on the property, or tenant injuries. Policies that cover property damage, liability protection, loss of rental income, and legal costs related to tenant litigation or property-related claims should be obtained by landlords. Landlords managing numerous rental properties may find that umbrella insurance plans or other coverage alternatives provide enhanced protections, reducing financial risk and protecting personal assets from lawsuits or property concerns.

Tenant screening and due diligence procedures are essential for assessing the creditworthiness, criminal history, rental history, and references of potential tenants to reduce the risk of property damage, defaulted leases, and tenant misbehavior. By fair housing rules, landlords must perform comprehensive background checks, confirm the sources of tenants' income, and evaluate each applicant's appropriateness using the rental application and screening standards. Landlords can pick trustworthy renters, reduce tenant turnover, and maintain occupancy levels that support property profitability and legal compliance in competitive rental markets using consistent screening procedures.

Landlords can obtain expert counsel on complex legal concerns, regulatory revisions, and landlord-tenant disputes by consulting real estate attorneys, housing authorities, or industry associations. Legal advisors ensure landlords uphold legal rights, protect property investments, and successfully handle legal obstacles by providing legal interpretations, drafting legal papers, negotiating settlements, and representing landlords in court proceedings or eviction cases. Landlords can obtain specialized expertise, reduce legal risks, and put proactive plans that support legal compliance and safeguard their interests in rental housing operations by speaking with legal specialists.

To navigate legal complexities, mitigate risks, and uphold ethical standards in property management operations, landlords and property managers must proactively comply with regulatory requirements, document practices, and insurance coverage, and seek professional legal guidance. Landlords can protect their property investments, reduce legal disputes, and promote lawful property management practices that support long-term rental property success and tenant satisfaction in various rental markets by being aware of their legal obligations, upholding legal compliance, and cultivating positive tenant relations.

CHAPTER X

Maximizing Returns and Expanding Your Portfolio

Strategies for increasing rental income

Strategic planning, proactive management, and taking advantage of growth possibilities to increase rental revenue and diversify property portfolios are all necessary to maximize profits on rental properties. In competitive rental markets, landlords and property investors can employ various tactics to boost rental income, maximize property performance, and meet financial objectives.

Market research, examining similar rental rates, and determining competitive rental prices that draw renters while optimizing property income potential are all necessary components of effective rental pricing strategies. To establish the ideal rent levels that compromise tenant affordability and property profitability, landlords should assess local market trends, demand-supply dynamics, neighborhood amenities, and property quality. Landlords can maintain competitive pricing strategies that maximize rental income and decrease vacancy rates in rental properties by adjusting rental prices based on market fluctuations, seasonal demand, property enhancements, or economic considerations.

Landlords can command higher rental rates and increase their property's appeal by investing in upgrades, renovations, and cosmetic improvements. Modernizing interior areas, installing energy-efficient fixtures, improving curb appeal, and upgrading kitchen equipment can all increase property value and justify price hikes, raising the possibility of rental income and tenant happiness. To optimize property value and rental revenue growth over time, landlords should prioritize low-cost renovations that yield a high return on investment (ROI), fit with tenant preferences, and adhere to building rules and permit requirements.

Providing extra facilities and services in competitive rental markets can set rental homes apart, draw in potential renters, and support higher rental rates. To cater to the convenience of tenants, their lifestyle choices, and their rental properties' general appeal, landlords might consider offering amenities like free utilities, parking lots, community leisure areas, laundry facilities, and pet-friendly regulations. Landlords can strategically invest in amenities that improve tenant satisfaction, increase the desirability of their property, and generate additional rental income streams that support long-term property profitability and tenant retention strategies by knowing their tenants' demographics, preferences, and lifestyle trends.

Landlords can capture additional rental income, modify rental pricing to reflect market conditions, and keep quality tenants in rental properties by strategically executing rent hikes and lease renewals. When negotiating lease terms, landlords should keep tenant affordability and landlord profitability in mind. They should also justify rental increases with prior notice and use property upgrades, market trends, inflationary considerations, or increased operating costs as justifications. By encouraging tenant retention, lowering turnover costs, and promoting steady rental revenue growth that eventually improves cash flow and real estate investment returns, landlords can offer incentives to renew their leases, such as longer lease terms, rental discounts, or property enhancements.

Enhancing rental income diversification, reducing investment risks, and maximizing portfolio growth opportunities are all achieved by diversifying investment portfolios through the acquisition of additional rental properties, the expansion of property holdings across various geographic locations, or the investment in a variety of property types (e.g., residential, commercial, multifamily). To finance property acquisitions, take advantage of market opportunities, and achieve economies of scale that maximize rental income streams, property value appreciation, and overall investment returns in dynamic real estate markets, landlords can make use of financing options, equity from existing properties, or real estate investment trusts (REITs).

Using proactive tenant and property maintenance tactics, effective property management practices maximize rental income, minimize vacancy rates, cut maintenance expenses, and optimize operating efficiencies. To maintain property condition, tenant satisfaction, and property value that supports ongoing rental income growth and investment profitability, landlords should prioritize responsive tenant communication, prompt property inspections, proactive maintenance schedules, and cost-effective repairs.

Landlords can maximize rental revenue potential and portfolio expansion by monitoring market trends, economic indicators, demographic shifts, and regulatory changes. This allows them to forecast market swings, alter rental methods, and seize emerging possibilities. Landlords can adjust rental pricing strategies, property management practices, and investment decisions that align with market demands, optimize property performance, and sustain long-term profitability in competitive rental markets by staying informed about industry trends, tenant preferences, and local market dynamics.

Diversifying your property portfolio

Expanding your investment holdings across several property types, regions, and market segments diversifies your property portfolio. This helps you reduce risk, maximize profits, and take advantage of various real estate opportunities. In the highly competitive real estate market, investors can accomplish sustainable growth and financial objectives by carefully diversifying their property portfolios, balancing income sources, and taking advantage of market dynamics.

Investors can diversify their property portfolios by obtaining various real estate assets, such as residential homes, commercial real estate, multifamily apartments, holiday rentals, industrial spaces, or mixed-use complexes. Each property has particular investment potential and characteristics related to renters, income streams, and market cycles to promote portfolio diversity, risk management, and long-term investment stability. Commercial assets offer lease flexibility, better rental yields, and business tenant stability, whereas residential properties offer consistent rental revenue and tenant demand. While vacation rentals cater to the short-term rental market and seasonal occupancy patterns, adding to the diversity of income sources and improving cash flow possibilities, multifamily apartments attract a wide range of tenant groups and produce ongoing rental income.

Acquiring properties across several towns, states, or nations is known as geographic diversity, and it helps lower the risks associated with investment concentration that arise from local market conditions, economic volatility, and legislative changes. Investing in various geographic areas enables one to profit from changes in the real estate market, demographic trends, and regional economic growth that affect property values, rental demand, and investment returns. Through diversifying property portfolios, investors can optimize property performance, reduce local market volatility, and strengthen portfolio resilience against external factors that could impact property values or rental income stability. This is achieved by allocating capital across various real estate assets with varying risk-return profiles, occupancy rates, lease terms, and property management requirements. Investors allocate resources to core, value-added, or opportunistic properties based on their investment objectives, risk tolerance, and market possibilities to maximize portfolio diversification, income production, and capital appreciation potential. In shifting market conditions, portfolio stability, liquidity, and overall investment performance are improved by balancing high-risk, high-reward investments and steady income-producing properties.

Diversified property portfolios reduce vacancy risks, maximize property occupancy rates across various asset classes, and produce diversified rental revenue streams, contributing to income stability and cash flow management. Properties that provide steady revenue provide a constant stream of cash flow to pay for mortgage payments, operational costs, and upkeep of the property, promoting long-term investment feasibility and financial sustainability. Investors can weather market changes, tenant turnover, and economic downturns with the income stability of diversified property portfolios, all while retaining rental income and protecting property value.

Monitoring property performance indicators, examining investment returns, and implementing proactive plans to improve tenant relations, portfolio diversity, and property value growth are all necessary components of effective portfolio management. To optimize investment returns, manage risks, and maintain long-term portfolio growth in dynamic real estate markets, investors should regularly review their portfolios, evaluate asset allocation strategies, and modify their investment approaches in response to market trends, economic indicators, and portfolio performance targets.

Scaling your investments sustainably

To build investment portfolios, maximize returns, and eventually reach financial objectives, scaling your real estate assets sustainably requires careful planning, cautious decision-making, and the utilization of growth prospects. Investors should promote ethical investing practices that enable long-term growth and resilience in the competitive real estate market while managing risk, improving asset performance, and capitalizing on market dynamics using sustainable scaling techniques.

Strategic investment planning that aligns with financial objectives, risk tolerance, and investment objectives is the first step toward sustainable scaling. To find growth prospects and maximize portfolio diversification, investors should specify their investment criteria, target property types, geographic preferences, and market sectors based on market research, economic projections, and industry trends. Investors can attain sustained investment returns and scalable growth in the real estate sector by devising well-defined investment strategies, capitalizing on developing market trends, and allocating capital efficiently.

Maximizing investment efficiency and growing investments sustainably depend on effective resource management and capital deployment. To finance real estate acquisitions, improvements, or development projects that raise property values, produce rental revenue, and facilitate portfolio expansion, investors should evaluate funding choices, use financial resources, and maximize capital allocation strategies. Investors can reduce liquidity risks, preserve investment flexibility, and take advantage of market opportunities consistent with long-term investment goals and sustainable growth strategies by carefully managing their financial resources.

Because portfolio diversity distributes investment risk over various asset classes, property kinds, and geographic regions, it is essential for scaling investments sustainably. Diversified portfolios improve investment resilience, lessen concentration risks related to specific properties or market segments, and lessen portfolio volatility during market or economic downturns. Investors seeking to maximize revenue streams, take advantage of various tenant demographics, and maintain long-term portfolio growth that underpins financial stability and investment performance ought to diversify across residential, commercial, multifamily, and niche real estate sectors.

Property management methods must achieve operational efficiency and scalability to maintain growth, maximize asset performance, and increase investment profitability. To reduce overhead expenses, boost tenant happiness, and optimize property revenue potential, investors should embrace cost-effective operational strategies, use technology solutions, and streamline property management operations. By implementing standardized management practices, outsourcing non-core activities, and allocating funds towards energy-efficient solutions or property upgrades, investors can optimize operational efficiencies throughout their investment portfolios, attract quality tenants, and achieve scalable growth.

By venturing into new markets, seizing growth prospects, and varying their investment portfolio, investors can achieve sustainable investment scaling by expanding their market presence and acquiring strategic properties. Investors should identify target markets, evaluate real estate investment opportunities, and negotiate advantageous real estate acquisitions that support portfolio expansion goals and investment criteria by conducting in-depth market research, assessing local market dynamics, and identifying emerging market trends. Investors can use market diversification techniques, economies of scale, and improved long-term investment performance and sustainability by proactively broadening their market reach.

Including environmental, social, and governance (ESG) factors in investment strategies increases asset value, encourages sustainable scaling techniques, and satisfies stakeholder expectations for ethical investing. Properties with energy-efficient renovations, green building certifications, and sustainable design elements should be given priority by investors to minimize their adverse environmental effects, cut running expenses, and draw in eco-aware renters. Investors can enhance tenant relationships, cultivate a positive brand reputation, and synchronize investment activities with sustainable development goals that support long-term growth and profitability in the real estate sector by implementing social responsibility initiatives, community engagement programs, and ethical business practices.

Long-term Wealth-building Strategies

To attain financial independence and accumulation over time, long-term wealth-building through real estate requires strategic planning, disciplined investing methods, and utilizing the unique advantages of property ownership. Using proactive wealth-building tactics, investors can take advantage of real estate's potential for asset appreciation, rental income generation, tax benefits, and portfolio diversification. This will help them establish lasting wealth and ensure their financial security.

Strategic investment planning that aligns with individual financial objectives, risk tolerance, and investment schedules is the first step toward developing long-term wealth. Investors had to specify their goals for the money, evaluate the market situation, and locate properties with growth potential for both capital gains and rental income. Investors can reduce investment risks, make well-informed decisions, and position themselves to take advantage of market opportunities supporting long-term wealth accumulation through strategic property acquisitions and portfolio diversification by conducting in-depth market research, evaluating economic indicators, and comprehending local market dynamics.

Real estate investments in rental properties that produce consistent rental income, stable cash flow, and financial independence offer prospects for passive income production. To diversify income streams, reduce investment risks, and use rental revenue to pay for property expenses, mortgage payments, and investment-related fees, investors can purchase residential, commercial, multifamily, or vacation rental properties. Through consistent rental income and passive income sources that support lifestyle flexibility and retirement planning, investors can maximize cash flow, meet financial goals, and build long-term wealth by optimizing rental pricing strategies, tenant management practices, and property maintenance efficiencies.

Long-term wealth-building methods benefit from the tax advantages and wealth preservation of real estate investments. To minimize taxable income and maximize cash flow, investors can deduct operating costs, property taxes, mortgage interest, and depreciation from rental income. Real estate investors can also take advantage of depreciation deductions that increase after-tax returns and preserve wealth over time, tax incentives for property enhancements or energy-efficient upgrades, and capital gains tax deferral through 1031 exchanges. Investors can reduce their tax obligations, protect their money, and reinvest their savings into more properties or wealth-building projects that can expedite portfolio growth and financial independence by utilizing tax-efficient investing tactics.

Managing risk well and diversifying your portfolio are crucial for creating long-term wealth through real estate investing. To reduce investment risks, balance income sources, and maximize investment returns, investors should diversify their property portfolios over various asset classes, geographical areas, and market segments. Diversification tactics distribute investment risk among properties, property kinds, and investment strategies that align with long-term wealth-building goals and financial objectives. This helps investors manage market volatility, economic downturns, or sector-specific hazards.

Real estate investments offer tangible assets, income-producing properties, and investment portfolios that may be passed down to future generations, which helps with legacy planning and generational wealth transfer. To leave a lasting legacy, protect family wealth, and ease wealth transfer, investors can set up trusts, use estate planning techniques, and take advantage of the advantages of property ownership. These strategies include succession planning, tax-efficient methods, and property management continuity that align with long-term financial objectives and personal values.

Real estate investment strategies that focus on long-term wealth building provide investors with a route to legacy planning, financial independence, asset appreciation, tax benefits, risk management, and portfolio diversification. Investors can achieve sustainable wealth growth, preserve investment capital, and ensure long-term financial stability while building a diversified real estate portfolio that supports lifestyle goals, retirement planning, and generational wealth transfer objectives by utilizing the unique advantages of real estate, making the most of investment opportunities, and adjusting to market dynamics.

CONCLUSION

In conclusion, "Unlocking Rental Wealth: Strategies for Successful Property Investment and Management" provides a comprehensive guide to navigating the complex yet rewarding world of rental property investment. Throughout this book, we have explored essential strategies for acquiring, managing, and maximizing the potential of rental properties to build sustainable wealth.

Key takeaways include the importance of thorough market research and property analysis before investing, understanding the financial aspects such as financing options and budgeting for renovations, and implementing effective property management practices to ensure tenant satisfaction and maintenance.

Moreover, the book emphasizes the significance of diversifying your portfolio across different types of properties or geographic locations to mitigate risks and optimize returns. It also underscores the role of continuous learning, adapting to market trends, and leveraging technology in enhancing operational efficiency and profitability.

Mastering these strategies empowers readers to make informed decisions, mitigate risks, and capitalize on opportunities in the dynamic real estate market. Whether you are a novice investor looking to start small or an experienced landlord aiming to expand your portfolio, "Unlocking Rental Wealth" is a practical roadmap for achieving long-term financial success through strategic property investment and management.

Ultimately, success in rental property investment requires diligence, patience, and a commitment to continuous improvement.

Thank you for buying and reading/ listening to our book. If you found this book useful/ helpful please take a few minutes and leave a review on the platform where you purchased our book. Your feedback matters greatly to us.